The Promise of
Christmas

Text copyright © Fleur Dorrell 2007
The author asserts the moral right
to be identified as the author of this work

Published by
The Bible Reading Fellowship
First Floor, Elsfield Hall
15–17 Elsfield Way, Oxford OX2 8FG
Website: www.brf.org.uk

ISBN 978 1 84101 214 8
First published 2007
10 9 8 7 6 5 4 3 2 1 0

Acknowledgments
Unless otherwise stated, scripture quotations are taken from the New
Jerusalem Bible, published and copyright © 1985 by Darton, Longman and
Todd Ltd and les Editions du Cerf, and by Doubleday, a division of Bantam
Doubleday Dell Publishing Group, Inc. Used by permission of Darton,
Longman and Todd Ltd, and Doubleday, a division of Random House, Inc.

Scriptures taken from The Holy Bible, New International Version, copyright
© 1973, 1978, 1984 by International Bible Society, are used by permission
of Hodder & Stoughton Limited. All rights reserved. 'NIV' is a registered
trademark of International Bible Society. UK trademark number 1448790.

A catalogue record for this book is available from the British Library

Printed in Singapore by Craft Print International Ltd

The Promise of
Christmas

Reflections for the Advent season

Fleur Dorrell

To my mother —
who always shows me the way to Christ

Contents

Introduction

Advent has been observed since at least the fourth century. Originally, it was a time when converts to Christianity prepared themselves for baptism. During the Middle Ages, it became associated with preparation for the second coming of Jesus. In early days it lasted from 11 November, the feast of St Martin, until Christmas Day, and was considered a pre-Christmas 'penitential season' when Christians devoted them-selves to prayer, fasting and almsgiving. In modern times, however, it has come to be seen as a time of anticipating the birth of Jesus and the celebrations of Christmas Day.

Advent comes from the Latin word for an 'arrival' or a 'coming', so 'Advent' means that the Lord is coming. Jesus came to Bethlehem at a specific time in history, about 2000 years ago. As the Alpha and Omega, he will come again to judge the living and the dead. He also comes to each of us in grace as our Saviour, speaking to us in our hearts. We can experience him in the eucharist and in the word of God proclaimed. Throughout our lives he comes to us in myriad ways, even in the people we meet and the experiences we have day by day, and we must be ready to receive and welcome him whenever he comes, however he comes.

At the moment, we live in an in-between period—between the two comings—and this waiting is at the heart of Advent. We wait in expectation since Christ, risen from the dead and now present among us in mystery, will be revealed to everyone on the last day as the glorious Son of our heavenly Father.

In this book we will be reflecting on the promises and prophecies throughout the Bible that prepare us for Christ's birth and mission on earth. We begin with creation, the promised land and the growth of the nation of Israel. We explore how God made covenants with his people and how they disobeyed him, and we are introduced to a number of prophets and their prophecies: what warnings and signs do they reveal to us in this season? To ensure that we don't stay in the past, we consider parallel politics and what they can teach us now, as well as promises by God of future hope and fulfilment in Christ.

These reflections affirm that Christ has come to us, that he is truly present in the world today and that he will come again in awesome power. During this Advent season, we celebrate God's incarnation, we hold on to our hope in his future kingdom and we know that one day we really will meet him in glory.

There are 25 short readings in this book, divided into five sections. You could read one every day from the first day of Advent or 1 December, whichever comes earlier. Alternatively, you could read in weekly sections, starting five weeks before Christmas. Before you begin each day, you may like to light a candle to still and centre your thoughts, and to be open to God's words speaking in your heart. When you are ready, you are invited to read through the scriptures and their reflections, to pause for the questions and then to say the final prayers when you feel it is right to finish.

There is a suggested image for each section that you may wish to look at if it helps you reflect during your Advent journey. These pictures can all be accessed on the Internet, or you can find them in art books in your local library. Suggested Internet links are given at the beginning of each new section.

❖

Promised land

Image of the week: Michelangelo's Creation of Adam,
Sistine Chapel, Rome

The first time the word 'Hebrew' is used in the Bible is
in Genesis 14:13, when Abram, now living near the
trees of Mamre in Hebron, is identified as 'Abram the
Hebrew'. The origin of the word is uncertain but is most
probably derived from a verb meaning 'to cross over a
boundary', so a Hebrew would be one who 'crossed
over' or went from place to place—a nomad, a wanderer
or an alien. This means that Joseph's description of
Palestine as 'the land of the Hebrews' in Genesis 40:15
was a deliberate paradox, for sojourners do not, by
definition, have or own land. Indeed, for 500 years, after
the time of Joseph, the people were Hebrews in the
'alien' sense of the word, living in the land of Egypt. So
when the Hebrew people eventually possessed the land
promised by God to the descendants of Abraham, Isaac
and Jacob, they would always be reminded by the root
meaning of their name, 'Hebrew', that the land was a
gift.

The notion of 'promised land' actually begins with
God's creation of a paradise in the garden of Eden, a
place where people could receive all of God's blessings

and walk in fellowship with him. This land of paradise was lost as a result of the Fall but a glimpse of restoration is found in the imagery of the promise made to Abraham (Genesis 13:15–17).

Even when the Israelites did take possession of the promised land after leaving Egypt, it was never owned by them but belonged to God. Under the laws set out in Leviticus 25:23, land could not be permanently bought or sold. It was never at the disposal of Israel for its national purposes. Instead, it was Israel that was at the disposal of God's purposes. The people remained tenants in God's land, bound by the terms of the covenant: if they were faithful to God, he would watch over them.

As the events of the Old Testament unfolded, the people rejected the terms of the covenant and defied God's love and concern. Even Solomon, at the zenith of his reign and power, went on to ruin things by importing foreign gods. In the end, fulfilling the warnings of Moses and other prophets, the people were dispossessed and driven out, exiled from the land that God had entrusted to their ancestors.

Jerusalem was safe from foreign armies as long as the *shekinah* or glory of God dwelt in her midst, in the temple. That is the significance of Ezekiel's visions in which, step by step, he sees the departure of God's glory from the city (Ezekiel 10:3–4, 18–19; 11:22–23). Once the glory had departed, Jerusalem was as vulnerable as any other place on earth. It was no longer a city under God's protection, and the exile and scattering of its people could not be averted.

The history of the Jewish people does not end with the exile, however. At God's appointed time, a remnant returned to part of the original territory and built a small replica of Solomon's temple. Even so, God's prophets were not distracted from their vision of the greatness of his redemptive work, painting a glorious picture of restoration. In Zechariah 2, for example, we read that Jerusalem shall be 'a city without walls', so expansive that it cannot be measured, and with a wall of fire around it (vv. 4–5, NIV). The reconstructed temple would manifest a greater glory than even Solomon's magnificent structure.

Thus the history of the relationship between God's pilgrim people and their promised land is a story enriched by the constant cycle of failure, rescue and newfound trust, through which God's faithfulness beckons his people into deeper commitment. During Advent we also are pilgrims, following the call to the same trust and commitment, by reflecting not just on the birth of Jesus Christ but on how he affects our life today, as individuals and as the Church.

Image of the week weblink

http://mv.vatican.va/3_EN/pages/x-Schede/CSNs/CSNs_V_StCentr_06.html

Light and life

In the beginning God created heaven and earth. Now the earth was a formless void, there was darkness over the deep, with a divine wind sweeping over the waters. God said, 'Let there be light,' and there was light. God saw that light was good, and God divided light from darkness. God called light 'day', and darkness he called 'night'. Evening came and morning came: the first day...

God said, 'Let there be lights in the vault of heaven to divide day from night, and let them indicate festivals, days and years. Let them be lights in the vault of heaven to shine on the earth.' And so it was. God made the two great lights: the greater light to govern the day, the smaller light to govern the night, and the stars. God set them in the vault of heaven to shine on the earth, to govern the day and the night and to divide light from darkness. God saw that it was good.

GENESIS 1:1–5, 14–18

'Genesis' in Greek means the beginning or the creation of something, and here we see the first book of the Bible describing the birth of our planet. Although our understanding of Christmas seems a million miles away from the beginning of the world, in one sense they are part of the same moment in God's time: think of Jesus saying in John 8:58 that 'before Abraham ever was, I am'. The same God who was at work revealing himself as Creator (and to the Israelites in the exodus) was again at work in human history, revealing himself in Jesus the Christ.

The Genesis account tells us that the earth was formed out of chaos, out of darkness. It is interesting that the same two Hebrew words translated as 'formless' and 'void' recur in the book of Jeremiah (4:22–23), when the prophet wants to warn Israel of their sins: '"My people are fools; they do not know me. They are senseless children; they have no understanding. They are skilled in doing evil; they know not how to do good." I looked at the earth, and it was formless and empty; and at the heavens, and their light was gone' (NIV).

Jeremiah is telling the Israelites that if they do not repent and turn back to God, they are unleashing chaos into the world, which will bring destruction and, in effect, reverse the creative activity of God, undoing the very work of creation.

In the Genesis story we also read of the 'divine wind' hovering or sweeping across the void; this wind will reappear often throughout biblical history and, indeed, in our own lives. It is the very Spirit of God, active in creation. We also notice the boundaries and order within God's perfect new creation. Each day is divided from the next and on each day something new is created that relates to the rest of creation; the seasons and years are also divided, so God presents us with a model of symbiosis as well as a work of exquisite art.

The idea of a world ordered by God who himself sets the limits and boundaries of his creation later becomes a fundamental principle for how humankind will relate to God. The idea of boundaries and limits as part of the created order provides the basis for the Israelites and us to develop systems of law and morality. This in turn reveals the inherent responsibilities and duties implicit in boundaries and limits, as we see later in the Genesis stories.

It has been asked which is more important: the sun or the moon, and some say the moon because you need the light at night to be able to see! Of course, it is a false question, because we need them both in different ways. For us believers, darkness is a metaphor for the absence of God, just as light is a symbol of his presence.

In the northern hemisphere, Advent is the season of winter darkness, which arrives like a heavy blanket weighing down upon the land; we turn back the clocks and the days become shorter. Yet the real darkness in our lives lies within the tragedies, the disasters and the sorrows we have to bear, both personally and globally. The times we live in can seem chaotic and dark.

The Israelites waited many centuries for the Messiah to deliver them, and they longed passionately for his coming. There are people today who also long for the Messiah but do not know where to find him, and they too feel the void, the long wait and the darkness in between. Yet the beginning of Genesis shows that we have light for the journey and an ordered framework in which to live. The lights and stars in the sky, so poetically described in the creation narrative, were the same lights, the same stars that would guide the wise men to baby Jesus. And if we set out this Advent in search of God, he will provide light for our journey too.

For reflection

Is there an aspect of your faith where there seems to be more darkness than light? Ask God to guide you through this darkness.

Prayer

Lord of all creation,
of the heavens and the earth,
this Advent bring to birth in me
the light I need to help me through the dark times. Amen

Let the children come

Then people brought little children to him, for him to lay his hands on them and pray. The disciples scolded them, but Jesus said, 'Let the little children alone, and do not stop them from coming to me; for it is to such as these that the kingdom of Heaven belongs.' Then he laid his hands on them and went on his way.

MATTHEW 19:13–15

Creation isn't just about the planet, it's about people; and Jesus' focus on children bridges the critical gap between the two, reminding us that children are the building blocks, the human components, of the future.

In biblical times (as in much of human history), children were regarded as insignificant. They had no power or status and were not even considered full or complete persons. It was considered important to have a large family of sons in order to continue the family line, and to be barren was deemed a curse. Even so, to embrace a child publicly was to embrace that which was unimportant, but Jesus purposely chose to do this.

In contrast to the discussion that the disciples had been sharing about who was the greatest, Jesus characterizes 'kingdom greatness' by showing them a helpless child (see Matthew 18:1–4). Only someone with a true servant's heart, willingly taking last place, could receive and value an insignificant child. Following Christ and denying ourselves involves becoming similarly insignificant and vulnerable because the kingdom of God does not play by human rules but by the rules of truth.

Another way of looking at the event in Matthew 19 is to wonder whether the disciples saw the children as infringing on their own time with Jesus. Even so, Jesus reacted strongly to their disapproval. Mark's account (10:13–16) says that he was 'indignant' on seeing how the disciples were trying to prevent children from meeting him. He was both grieved and angry and immediately set about challenging and correcting the disciples. This attitude must surely have confused his followers because, if they considered time spent with children as wasted whereas Jesus seem to consider it invaluable, then what was really going on? What might the implications be for other areas of the disciples' understanding, their relations with other social and religious groups? The way that Jesus kept turning the disciples' minds and hearts upside down must have been unsettling, not to say frightening. It would have left them unsure about their role in society and about how their faith should be practised.

In God's eyes, no time or energy invested in bringing children to Jesus was ever wasted. We should also develop this attitude if we don't already have it. We want children to expect our attention, time and involvement in their lives and thoughts because, in providing these things, we serve them in Christ's name. By doing what we can to help bring children to Christ, we can be their heralds of the gospel, trusting that it will bear fruit in their lives. As we do this, we mirror the care for children shown by Jesus himself. Working with children in Sunday school or in preschool care or primary education can be part of bringing children to Christ. We must also be ready for the heart-searching questions and inquisitiveness that children bring with them. Children tend to see God more clearly than adults because they have less mental and emotional baggage.

Jesus purposely chose to come into this world as an infant and not as an adult. Since he knew what it was to be a child, how could he treat other children with anything less than the total dignity that all creation deserves? This Advent, let us reflect on how children can show us the way to Christ and how they will always continue to challenge us in our beliefs. The challenge is part of their journey and our journey too, as we continue to seek to know God more.

For reflection

Has a child—or a simple, direct question from an adult—ever challenged your faith? Did you feel you responded as a 'herald of the gospel'?

Prayer

Loving God,
You gave us your Son as a baby in a manger.
May his vulnerability humble us.
Let us pray for all those children
who have no parents to care for them,
and ask that your love will give them hope. Amen

A tower of faith?

The whole world spoke the same language, with the same vocabulary. Now, as people moved eastwards they found a valley in the land of Shinar where they settled. They said to one another, 'Come, let us make bricks and bake them in the fire.' For stone they used bricks, and for mortar they used bitumen. 'Come,' they said, 'let us build ourselves a city and a tower with its top reaching heaven. Let us make a name for ourselves, so that we do not get scattered all over the world.'

Now Yahweh came down to see the city and the tower that the people had built. 'So they are all a single people with a single language!' said Yahweh. 'This is only the start of their undertakings! Now nothing they plan to do will be beyond them. Come, let us go down and confuse their language there, so that they cannot understand one another.' Yahweh scattered them thence all over the world, and they stopped building the city. That is why it was called Babel, since there Yahweh confused the language of the whole world; and from there Yahweh scattered them all over the world.

GENESIS 11:1–9

The appearance of the first city after the flood illustrates the hunger of humankind to huddle together for companionship as they try to rebuild their lives. It's a sort of 'safety and pleasure in numbers' approach. Cities are centres of life, of events; they are the commercial providers where all the needs of the body can be met. They are places of pleasure and fun, where people think that all the hungers of the soul can be satisfied: for beauty, art, music and all the ingredients of culture.

The tower, on the other hand, is designed to be a religious building, intending to open humankind to the mysteries of the heavens, emulating the greatness of God. The people would also have admired its architectural greatness, as it would have been a colossal enterprise to build and they may have conceived of it as reaching into the heavens.

There was a problem, though, made clear in the words, 'Let us make a name for ourselves, so that we do not get scattered all over the world'. God had told the descendants of Noah to 'increase in number and fill the earth' (Genesis 9:1, NIV), a reiteration of the command originally given to Adam and Eve in Genesis 1:28. The settlement of Shinar (the plain where the tower was built) could be construed as a partial fulfilment of that command. Yet, as we read on, we find that the goal of this particular settlement was not to fulfil God's command but to defy it. From the beginning, Babylon's goal was to resist any further scattering of the peoples over the earth and instead to create a city where the achievements of a united and integrated people would be centralized and celebrated.

They did not want to build God's city but to establish a reputation for themselves and, more than that, create for themselves independence from God. Accordingly, God very sensibly decides that the people should be further dispersed and their languages muddled. Many centuries later, the day of Pentecost gave a foretaste of the reversal of this moment, when God's Holy Spirit came down as tongues of fire and the disciples received the gift of speaking in languages that everyone could understand (Acts 2:5–6).

In today's world, globalization can be seen as a corollary of the story of Babel, bringing people together and unifying their connections and relationships. And, as we see today, globalization can have a negative impact when it becomes a case of centralizing power and creating uniformity as dictated by the most powerful, rather than promoting fairness and equality of opportunity.

Advent can help us to broaden our horizons, to look at life from God's perspective. The 'towers' we build even in God's name may be built on the wrong foundations, or for the wrong purpose, so during this season let us ask God to give us discernment about our own projects and agendas. What are the places in our lives where we most experience God's presence? Let us cherish these places, for they are holy ground.

For reflection

Are there any 'towers' in your life that should be dismantled?

Prayer

Lord of all dimensions,
show me the places in my life
where I can draw closest to you.
May I always find in you
my true tower of strength. Amen

The parting of the waves

Then Moses stretched out his hand over the sea, and Yahweh drove the sea back with a strong easterly wind all night and made the sea into dry land. The waters were divided and the Israelites went on dry ground right through the sea, with walls of water to right and left of them. The Egyptians gave chase, and all Pharaoh's horses, chariots and horsemen went into the sea after them... That day, Yahweh rescued Israel from the clutches of the Egyptians, and Israel saw the Egyptians lying dead on the sea-shore. When Israel saw the mighty deed that Yahweh had performed against the Egyptians, the people revered Yahweh and put their faith in Yahweh and in Moses, his servant.

EXODUS 14:21–23, 30–31

There is a greeting card in the shops that shows Moses frustratedly trying to lead the Israelites through the Red Sea. They are hesitant and complaining, and the caption underneath says, 'What do you mean—it's a bit muddy?' People were as doubtful then as they are now about faith and its difficulties, its utter messiness, even when the opportunity for deliverance from years of oppression is open right in front of them.

Moses, as we know, was drawn out of the water and the bulrushes as a baby (Exodus 2:5–6), and Moses is an Egyptian name meaning 'to be drawn out' (v. 10). He grows up to fulfil his own name, drawing the Israelites out of water to safety from the oppressive Egyptians. In this story, the sea is the instrument of God's wrath, destroying the Egyptians, and it is also the instrument of Israel's deliverance. Can we see here a foreshadowing of the waters of baptism, another symbol of cleansing and deliverance?

This episode of the Israelites passing through the Red Sea shows us that things are not always what they seem. The Israelites were afraid, assuming that the Egyptians would be victorious over them. The Egyptians, on the other hand, were confident, assuming that they would soon recapture the Israelites and take them back to Egypt as their slaves. But both Egyptians and Israelites were wrong in their limited understanding of events. Confident as they were, the Egyptians died in the sea and, afraid as the Israelites were, they passed through the sea, miraculously delivered from their enemies. Although the Egyptians had the artillery, the chariots and the soldiers, they failed to comprehend that they were confronting God and his chosen people.

The Israelites were so afraid that they would have considered returning to Egypt (14:11–12), but God had promised to deliver them safely to the promised land. God also assured the Israelites of his presence and guidance by an accompanying pillar of cloud and fire (13:21–22). No people were more secure than the Israelites, no matter how the situation appeared. Along with generations of Jewish people since then, we can view the exodus not simply as a distant event in the past, but rather as a model for understanding the experience of God's salvation for all time. It is a pattern of freedom:

distress followed by unexpected deliverance, which demands a response from us.

In life we have our own Red Seas to cross and our own Pharaoh-like armies to face—seemingly impossible situations at home or at work. God calls us to stand firm, like Moses, and to trust in him. We may experience miracles or we may not, we may witness great wonders in our own lives or we may not, but what matters is that we stick with God who, in the long run, will wash away all our pain.

He will stop our Pharaohs and open our Red Seas, but we must walk the same path of obedience as the Israelites, all the way through the desert to the promised land. Like them, we must take small, muddy and dangerous steps into a very strange land.

Advent is marked by this same spirit of expectation, of anticipation, of longing, of promise. There is a yearning for deliverance first expressed by the Israelites in Egypt as they cried out under oppression. It is the cry of those who have experienced injustice and yet have hope of deliverance. This Advent, Jesus comes again to give us that hope of freedom found only in him. The steps are just as muddy and just as dangerous but we need to take them if we are to grow in Christian maturity.

For reflection

Do you believe that God can provide deliverance—and are you willing to follow his directions?

Prayer

Lord of the mighty waves,
in the tides and trials of my life
teach me how to walk in faith
that I will know the life-giving strength of your truth. Amen

Created in Christ

He is the image of the unseen God,
the first-born of all creation,
for in him were created all things
in heaven and on earth:
everything visible and everything invisible,
thrones, ruling forces, sovereignties, powers—
all things were created through him and for him.
He exists before all things
and in him all things hold together,
and he is the Head of the Body,
that is, the Church.
He is the Beginning,
the first-born from the dead,
so that he should be supreme in every way;
because God wanted all fullness to be found in him
and through him to reconcile all things to him,
everything in heaven and everything on earth,
by making peace through his death on the cross.

COLOSSIANS 1:15–20

At the end of this first section of Advent readings, it is appropriate to culminate with a hymn to the role of Christ in creation. This rich poem hints at Wisdom motifs used in the Old Testament, such as in Proverbs 3:19, where Wisdom is described as an agent in creation. The earthly powers or angels are described as subordinate to Christ, to combat the contemporary thinking in Colossae that they might be rivals of Christ, able to contribute to or take away from his power. Such beliefs grew out of a culture where people worshipped a number of different deities simultaneously.

Paul here is up against a problem that emerged time and again over the course of biblical history: a monotheistic faith just didn't seem sufficiently attractive. The whole of the Old Testament grapples with the conflict between the worship of the one true God and the fact that the Israelites repeatedly sought a variety of gods and goddesses. The prophets constantly reminded the people that Yahweh was their only God—and here again we see Paul reminding the Colossians that God is number one. Jesus is Lord over all other divine beings; genuine power comes only from God and we are arrogant if we think we know better and dare to ignore the supremacy of Christ.

We may not think that we are tempted to worship other divine beings, but what about today's obsessive shopping culture? Globalization has provided us with even more reasons to buy what we like, when we like and from where we like, regardless of those who have to make and sell these products. Is this our modern-day idolatry?

The imagery of royalty and sovereignty in our Bible passage is also important in this Advent season. The Jewish people had been waiting for the Messiah to come as a king, but they failed to see that their idea of kingship was thoroughly different from that of Jesus. As a result, they misunderstood his surrender to the cross (and his poverty-stricken birth). Jesus' kingship was rooted in humility, as well as in his power over death.

Paul's poem is like a medieval tapestry, with two panels telling one story, drawing together the inter-linked threads of the 'first-born of all creation' and the 'first-born from the dead'. The title 'first-born' has a rich significance, especially when considered against an Old Testament context. The first-born son was traditionally the heir to the majority or all of his father's property, so Paul is acknowledging Jesus as heir of the world from the beginning, and considers the lavish extent of his reign over everything. All creation was made for God's own Son.

At the same time, the cross was known to Jesus, the first-born, from all eternity and, as the first-born, Jesus knew and accepted the cost of his inheritance. Christ's role places him not only as the head of a new race, but also as the elder brother of his people. Amazingly, we have become brothers and sisters of the sovereign first-born. We have inherited eternal life because the first-born has shared his inheritance with us.

Paul's poem eloquently reminds us how Jesus is 'before all things' both in time and in dignity. As the first-born is also preeminent over his new creation, we learn a healthy lesson for the Church here: to stop trying to run things our way and conform to our own limited model. If the Church is the inheritance of Jesus Christ, then let him be Lord! He will not give her up, nor will he sell his birthright to any angel, dictator, human or devil. For the Church during this Advent, as well as for you and me, this is both a striking warning and a profound comfort.

For reflection

What types of 'idols' do you find yourself worshipping in your daily life?

Prayer

God of true royalty,
show me your throne of righteousness
and your sceptre of truth.
May I kneel before you in humble adoration. Amen

Broken promises

*Image of the week: the 'Daily bread' stained-glass
window at Durham Cathedral*

The Bible speaks of a number of different covenants that
God made with Israel. There was one with Abraham
(Genesis 17), with Moses (Deuteronomy 5, which in-
cludes the Ten Commandments) and with David (2
Samuel 7), as well as one that is found in the book of
Jeremiah, where God promises forgiveness to his people
(ch. 31).

The history of the Old Testament is the history of
how this series of covenants was renewed and re-
adjusted. The Hebrew term for covenant (*berit*) seems
to have the root meaning of 'bond', indicating a
binding relationship; the idea of 'binding, putting
together' is also suggested in the Greek term *syntheke*.
Another term used in the New Testament is *diatheke*
('will, testament'), pointing more to the legal aspect of
a covenant. Taking the various meanings together, in
general (both in ancient civilizations and today), a
covenant signifies a relationship based on commitment, which includes both promises and obligations
and is distinguished by reliability and endurance. The
relationship is usually sealed by a rite, such as an oath,

sacred meal, blood sacrifice or invocation of blessings and curses.

The covenants between God and the people are all marked by divine favour or grace; in Hebrew the word used is *hesed*, which means 'loving-kindness'. These covenants express God's commitment and faithfulness and therefore establish an ongoing relationship. They differ from one another to the degree by which they are dependent upon the people's response, which is inevitably subject to human weakness and sin. The covenants with Abraham and David have a stronger flavour of 'everlasting covenant' because they rely upon divine grace alone and are not conditional on human behaviour.

These two covenants include divine promises: for Abraham, this meant the land as an everlasting possession, and a special relationship between God and the descendants of Abraham and Sarah (Genesis 17:7–8). Similarly, the covenant with David does not impose legal conditions, but offers a gracious promise of an unbroken succession of kings upon the throne of David. Although unfaithful kings will be chastised if they behave badly while in post, God will not withdraw the covenant promises of grace made to David (Psalm 89).

On the other hand, the covenant with Moses, as detailed in Deuteronomy, has a strong conditional note, as its sustainability is based on the people's obedience to the covenant criteria. If the people are unfaithful, they will be punished. Carried to the extreme, this covenant could be annulled, so that no longer would Yahweh be their God and no longer would Israel be God's people (see Hosea 1:9). The renewal of the covenant would be based solely on God's forgiving grace (Exodus 34:6–9; Jeremiah 31:31–33; Ezekiel 16:59–63).

The New Testament draws upon all of these covenant traditions. Paul's interpretation of the new relationship between God and people, shown by the display of God's grace in Jesus Christ, sent him back beyond the Mosaic covenant of obligation to the Abrahamic covenant of promise (see Galatians 3:6–18). The Davidic covenant, especially as expressed in the prophecies of the book of Isaiah (see 9:5–6 and 49:8), provided a theological context for the announcement that Jesus is the Messiah (Christ), the Son of God.

Taken together, these covenants in both the Old and New Testaments are pertinent to the Advent season in their emphasis on a binding relationship and a future promise. Throughout Advent, by praying and reading the scriptures daily, and pondering Christ's coming birth, we too are binding our hearts and preparing ourselves for his journey into this world; we too are awaiting a promise of fulfilment by renewing our relationship with him each and every Advent. And, as he does with all the previous covenants, God again keeps his promise and we are filled with renewed grace in his Son.

Image of the week weblink

www.durhamcathedral.co.uk/introduction/gallery/daily_bread

In the image of God

God said, 'Let us make man in our own image, in the likeness of ourselves, and let them be masters of the fish of the sea, the birds of heaven, the cattle, all the wild animals and all the creatures that creep along the ground.' God created man in the image of himself, in the image of God he created him, male and female he created them…

Yahweh God took the man and settled him in the garden of Eden to cultivate and take care of it. Then Yahweh God gave the man this command, 'You are free to eat of all the trees in the garden. But of the tree of the knowledge of good and evil you are not to eat; for, the day you eat of that, you are doomed to die.'

Yahweh God said, 'It is not right that the man should be alone. I shall make him a helper.'

GENESIS 1:26–27; 2:15–18

Although the Christmas veneration of the evergreen tree is firmly rooted in pre-Christian traditions, Christmas trees have two interesting Christian traditions linked to them. During the 14th and 15th centuries, evergreens with apples hung from their boughs (instead of the winter-bare branches of a real apple tree) played an important role in the miracle plays presented in or outside churches on 24 December, Christmas Eve. In the early church calendar of saints, Christmas Eve was Adam and Eve's Day, the occasion for a play depicting the dramatic events concerning the fruit tree in the garden of Eden. In many cities, the actors paraded through the streets before the performance, with the actor playing Adam carrying the 'Paradise Tree'.

Since this tree was the only prop on the stage during the play, it gained a lasting association with Christmas long after the medieval plays were no longer performed. By the 17th century, evergreens hung with apples were no longer considered merely as trees of temptation and were traditionally decorated each Christmas, although as late as the latter part of the 19th century people in northern Germany still bought little figures of Adam and Eve and the serpent to put under their 'Tree of Life'.

The Bible account is about Adam and Eve's disobedience in their deal with God. There was nothing essentially evil about the tree or the fruit of the tree. Rather, it was the act of disobedience that opened human eyes to evil. Their disobedience brought sin and evil into their lives—and into the world. Sadly, the tree may well have been acceptable to eat, but at a later time. They were not ready to handle it appropriately. Similarly, many of us may find ourselves in situations that we are not ready to handle but that, in time, we can deal with wisely.

Sceptics often complain that God set up Adam and Eve to fail—but he had to give them a choice. Without the free will to choose, they would have been mere puppets or robots: where would be the humanity in that? God wanted Adam and Eve to choose to love and trust him, and the only way to give them this choice was to show them what was not allowed. Adam and Eve had plenty to eat and could have chosen to obey God without yielding to their curiosity. So why did they disobey and what did they think they would gain by listening to the snake?

Have you ever wondered what would have happened if Adam and Eve had never eaten of that tree? Imagine the world without shame and disgrace, bitterness and envy, hatred, violence, anger, pride and selfishness. We could enjoy the glory of the Lord all day long, and discover and learn and grow endlessly in the knowledge and wisdom and love of God. We may regret what Adam did, but all too often we choose to repeat his mistake, when we heed the voice of so-called independent reason above the true voice of God.

The apostle Paul identifies Christ as the new Adam (1 Corinthians 15:45) and contrasts him with the first Adam. While the disobedience of the first Adam resulted in sin and death, the saving work of Jesus Christ, the new Adam, redeemed humanity and offers to all the grace and gift of eternal life (Romans 5:15). We know that one day God will make all things new, restoring the damage done to creation by the fall. Yet, even now, by repenting of our rebellion against God and by turning to Jesus, the tree of life, our relationship with God can be restored here and now to what it should always have been. And, through our submission and obedience, Jesus Christ can extend his blessing to others.

For reflection

Do you see yourself as rebelling against God or in relationship with him?

Prayer

God, creator of paradise,
may my curiosity not blind me
to the gifts you have already given me.
May I be content in myself,
not searching for that which I cannot handle. Amen

Stars and sand

Yahweh said to Abram, 'Leave your country, your kindred and your father's house for a country which I shall show you; and I shall make you a great nation, I shall bless you and make your name famous; you are to be a blessing! I shall bless those who bless you, and shall curse those who curse you, and all clans on earth will bless themselves by you.'

GENESIS 12:1–3

'I will shower blessings on you and make your descendants as numerous as the stars of heaven and the grains of sand on the seashore.'

GENESIS 22:17

The biblical idea of covenant was a novel element in the religion of ancient Israel: the people were bound in relationship to the one God, Yahweh, who made an exclusive or 'jealous' claim upon their loyalty. In a larger sense, the relationship between all creatures and their Creator is expressed in the universal covenant with Noah (Genesis 9:1–17), which assures God's faithful pledge to humankind, to animals and to the earth itself. Later in the book of Genesis, however, the main emphasis is given to God's covenant with the Israelite people, beginning with the migration of Abraham and

Sarah in response to God's call and the promise of a special relationship between God and their descendants, as seen in today's passages. This covenant with the ancestor of Israel is the prelude to the crucial events of the exodus and all that follows as the nation is established. The blessing comes to final fruition in the birth of Christ, part of the line of Abraham through Isaac, Jacob and King David.

Some of Abraham's associates and neighbours believed that their god was in a particular rock. Others worshipped on a particular mountain. As these people travelled away from that rock or that mountain, they thought that they were moving further away from their god. Yahweh, however, wanted Abraham to know that he was the God of all places and times. Abraham could worship God no matter where God led him, and his conversation with God could continue uninterrupted, no matter the location, under any circumstances.

Like Abraham and Sarah, we may be feeling for whatever reason that we have stepped out of the known world into a desert where all directions look the same. Yet, although we do not know where we are heading and although we have no map, we may feel ourselves inexorably drawn forward by a voice that calls us by name. The desert still surrounds us. We cannot see any path except the one we ourselves make, step by step. Behind us, the way we have travelled appears to be swallowed in shifting sands, but where we stand right now is the very spot where God has called us to be. Like Abraham, we can hear God's call.

The imagery of the stars and sand is particularly

evocative in our Bible passage because, with both these natural phenomena, we have no way of calculating their number or immensity: they are too great for us to contain in our finite minds. How like God's immensity! And just as sand lies on the ground beneath our feet and stars are scattered across the sky, so we can think of our Creator God encompassing us; whichever direction we look, we are still surrounded by his loving care and his guiding hand.

As well as receiving the promised miracle of a family, Abram was later tested to the limit when he was asked to sacrifice his only son to God (Genesis 22:1–14). It is very difficult to understand this episode: why would God command such a cruel act? Perhaps the answer is revealed not so much in the sacrificial testing but in identifying who is in control of our lives. No matter how blessed we are throughout our lives, it is God who can both give and take away, with or without warning.

The whole of Israelite history pivoted around the covenants that God kept faithfully but that his people inevitably failed to keep. This tension reaches its dramatic climax in the crucifixion, when God sends his own Son to be sacrificed for our sins. In contrast to the near-sacrifice of Abraham's son Isaac, Jesus' sacrifice is literally carried through and therefore fulfils its purpose. Thus this season of Advent is not just about looking forward to Jesus' birth, but also anticipates God's ultimate covenantal gift to all of us—the sacrifice of his very Son on earth.

For reflection

In what ways have you been blessed by God?

Prayer

God of all generations,
thank you for the blessing of my life.
May I be willing to make whatever sacrifices you ask
and thereby learn the true cost of discipleship. Amen

Tenderness and compassion

Yahweh said to Moses, 'Cut two tablets of stone like the first ones and come up to me on the mountain, and I will write on the tablets the words that were on the first tablets, which you broke. Be ready at dawn; at dawn come up Mount Sinai and wait for me there at the top of the mountain. No one may come up with you, no one may be seen anywhere on the mountain; the flocks and herds may not even graze in front of this mountain.' So he cut two tablets of stone like the first and, with the two tablets of stone in his hands, Moses went up Mount Sinai in the early morning as Yahweh had ordered. And Yahweh descended in a cloud and stood with him there and pronounced the name Yahweh. Then Yahweh passed before him and called out, 'Yahweh, Yahweh, God of tenderness and compassion, slow to anger, rich in faithful love and constancy, maintaining his faithful love to thousands, forgiving fault, crime and sin, yet letting nothing go unchecked.'

EXODUS 34:1–7

In the Judeo-Christian tradition, there are four main sacred mountains in the Middle East: Mount Ararat in eastern Turkey, the traditional landing place of Noah's ark; Mount Sinai in the Sinai peninsula, the peak where Moses received the Ten Commandments; Mount Zion in Israel, where the city of Jerusalem lies; and Mount

Tabor, also in Israel, the site of the transfiguration of Jesus. Mount Sinai, also called Horeb and Jebel Musa (the mountain of Moses) is still a popular pilgrimage destination, which now includes the Monastery of St Catherine and the alleged site of the burning bush.

The covenant that God made with Moses at Sinai was part of the long journey to the promised land, made even longer by the intransigence and stubbornness of the Israelites who, in tasting freedom, became so in-toxicated with it that they lost their bearings. And so in the Mosaic covenant we find rules for a whole way of life set down in great detail, providing safeguards and protection for this new relationship between God and the people.

This covenant is not a pact between equals; it is analogous to the treaties of vassalage common at the time (unequal relationships between different states, based on the domination of one nation by another). Yahweh decides to establish this allegiance to Israel by dictating his own conditions, seen most clearly in the Ten Commandments. It is interesting to consider how great the impact of these commandments has been on societies, whether Christian or not. They certainly form the basis of much legislation in the developed world and, when we consider other world religions, most have a set of moral codes that have striking parallels with several of these commandments.

The commandments should not, however, be seen in isolation from the rest of our faith, as a mere rule book. If that happens, they become divorced from their principle aim—that of salvation. The covenant between

Yahweh and the Israelites was an essential part of God's plan of salvation and grace, but unfortunately the people did not keep their side of the deal. Through their disobedience the covenant was actually annulled, and Moses graphically represented this by smashing the first tablets of stone (Exodus 32:19). After Moses pleads on the people's behalf, Yahweh relents and renews the covenant. Then Moses the mediator goes to meet God on the holy mountain and hears the divine proclamation of forgiveness, justice and mercy in the Bible passage above.

The cloud (34:5) was the immediate and visible presence and power of God: since humans were not worthy to face God in the flesh, Yahweh appeared in different forms, such as this cloud. He also descended as a cloud to cover the entrance to the tabernacle, the tent made under divine orders to be a dwelling place for God (and a place to keep the stone tablets and other sacred objects) as the people went on their way through the desert (see 40:34). God continued to be with them, in the centre of their camp, even after they had left Mount Sinai behind.

It is interesting that Luke uses a word for 'cloud' with an equivalent root meaning when he writes about the Holy Spirit's 'overshadowing' of Mary in his account of the annunciation (Luke 1:35). The angel Gabriel was clearly drawing a parallel between God's presence in the old tabernacle and in Mary as the new, living tabernacle, chosen to bear the Messiah. The difference is that, this time, under the new covenant, the promise of salvation is for everyone who believes in Christ, the perfect and holy sacrifice, with whom no other earthly object of worship can ever compare.

For reflection

This Advent, how can we be more tender, compassionate, slow to anger, rich in faithful love, constant and forgiving of our own and others' faults?

Prayer

Lord of the mountains,
help me to understand the height and depth of your laws,
and help me to understand how they demonstrate
the warmth of your love and constancy.
Wherever you call my name,
I want to meet you there. Amen

In your hearts
and in your homes

'Let these words of mine remain in your heart and in your soul; fasten them on your hand as a sign and on your forehead as a headband. Teach them to your children, and keep on telling them, when you are sitting at home, when you are out and about, when you are lying down and when you are standing up. Write them on the doorposts of your house and on your gates, so that you and your children may live long in the country which Yahweh swore to your ancestors that he would give them for as long as there is a sky above the earth.'

DEUTERONOMY 11:18–21

The 'words' that we are asked here to put in our hearts and bind on our hands are the Ten Commandments: this passage of Deuteronomy occurs immediately after the account of how the commandments were written on new tablets of stone and presented again to the people. Over time, however, the 'words' came to mean the whole law of the Lord. To put these words into our heart and soul means to read, remember, learn and absorb all the commandments of God, so that we instinctively know the right course of action in every situation.

It is less clear, though, what it means to fasten these words as a sign on our hand and as a headband on our forehead. It became Jewish custom to write out Hebrew texts from Exodus and Deuteronomy in tiny print on minuscule scrolls of paper, which were then placed in little black leather boxes called phylacteries and bound with leather straps around the head and the right arm. Thus the words of the Lord were, quite literally, bound to the hand and fixed to the forehead. The command also urges the writing of these words on the doorposts of house and gates, and this was interpreted by attaching similar scrolls in containers (*mezuzot*) over the entrance to houses.

This way of engaging with the word of God might seem strange to us. After all, how can nailing a scroll over the door help us to get the law of the Lord into our hearts? In fact, it is an outward reminder of an inner truth. In the New Testament, Jesus suggests that we fulfil the commandments by taking them to heart. Despite outwardly good deeds, our hearts may not be pure. We may not commit murder, but we may still harbour anger in our hearts, so that we are obeying the letter but not the spirit of God's law (Matthew 5:21–22). Jesus turned away those who claimed to have done good deeds in his name and those who were outwardly righteous but in fact full of anger and bitterness.

Jesus therefore takes the Deuteronomy text one stage further by making a distinction between hearing and knowing the words of the law and actually doing what they say. For Jesus, all the Old Testament commandments are summed up in two: love the Lord your God, and love your neighbour as yourself (Matthew 22:37–40). For all of us, it is by actually doing works of love, even when we do not feel love in our hearts, that we can change the way we think and feel. It is by doing what we know to be right, especially when we don't feel like doing it, that our hand begins to teach our heart.

To act with gentleness when we are angry, to give of our time and resources when we are feeling selfish, to behave humbly when pride or fear is in our heart and to listen when we would rather speak are all acts that change us each day. They will turn our anger to gentleness, our selfishness into generosity, our pride and fear into humility. So let us therefore not only put these commandments into our hearts, but also let us 'bind them to our hands'—and not just our hands, because there is more to behaviour than what we might think of as 'doing'. We also relate to others in what we say, how we judge and discern, what we choose to hear and read. Wearing a cross around our neck or a fish badge upon our lapel, and hanging icons and other religious images in our homes, can help to 'bind' the commandments to our hearts and remind us that what we do and what we focus on can change who we are.

Remembering God's commandments is depicted as a form of divine discipline, a kind of worship that also includes our children. It therefore points beyond us to those who will be the inheritors of our faith. One of the problems in our Western culture is that this faith and these stories and commandments have not continued to be handed from one generation to another, have not been retold and shared widely enough among younger people. The fact that so many Western people do not know the most famous Bible stories, and may not even know that Christmas is about Jesus' birth, suggests not illiteracy but lack of faith education. Advent is an ideal time to focus on retelling the story of our faith and passing on our Christian beliefs to others.

For reflection

How is your faith written into your heart and soul?

Prayer

God of my home and of my gate,
breathe your love into my heart.
Melt my anger, my pride and my selfishness—
so that your words are written in the centre of my life.
Amen

A new spirit

'Look, the days are coming, Yahweh declares, when I shall make a new covenant with the House of Israel (and the House of Judah), but not like the covenant I made with their ancestors the day I took them by the hand to bring them out of Egypt, a covenant which they broke, even though I was their Master, Yahweh declares. No, this is the covenant I shall make with the House of Israel when those days have come, Yahweh declares. Within them I shall plant my Law, writing it on their hearts. Then I shall be their God and they will be my people. There will be no further need for everyone to teach neighbour or brother, saying, "Learn to know Yahweh!" No, they will all know me, from the least to the greatest, Yahweh declares, since I shall forgive their guilt and never more call their sin to mind.'

JEREMIAH 31:31–34

'I shall pour clean water over you and you will be cleansed; I shall cleanse you of all your filth and of all your foul idols. I shall give you a new heart, and put a new spirit in you; I shall remove the heart of stone from your bodies and give you a heart of flesh instead. I shall put my spirit in you, and make you keep my laws, and respect and practise my judgments. You will live in the country which I gave your ancestors. You will be my people and I shall be your God.'

EZEKIEL 36:25–28

Jeremiah began his ministry in Jerusalem around 627BC and witnessed the final years of Jerusalem before it fell to Nebuchadnezzar in 597BC. His preaching appears to indicate that the reforms by King Josiah (see 2 Kings 23:4–25) had been unsuccessful, because his preaching calls the people back to faithful worship of Yahweh.

Jeremiah affirms that the Israelites can rely on the promise that God will build them up again. They have learnt that they cannot restore themselves. Instead, they have to rely on God totally, and God's everlasting love for his people can bring them back even from the disaster of Babylonian exile. God will make a new covenant, which is written on their hearts, unlike the old Mosaic covenant that was written in stone.

In Hebrew, the 'heart' represents not so much emotion as the seat of practical knowledge, and is not significantly different from 'mind'. The image of the heart identifies the new covenant relationship with God as an internal matter rather than one that is purely external. Each person, regardless of social status, will have a personal knowledge of God, not dependent on the instruction of a friend, relative or neighbour—or even Moses or the prophets! The people have proved unable to keep the covenant set up at Sinai in which they promised to be God's people, so to hear these words promising a new relationship with God must have been an extraordinary relief and a spiritual liberation.

The act of forgiveness is always initiated by God, and here it has no explicit requirement of repentance. The theology of the law written on the heart implies that Israel will not be able to break the law in the future because it is no longer an external requirement. The law becomes synonymous with 'knowing God', which means having such a close relationship with God that people would behave appropriately most or all of the time. If all people lived by grace, there would be no need of laws because everyone would know how to behave righteously—and would want to do so.

In our passage from Ezekiel, the sprinkling of water and the action of the Spirit are both actions carried out by God. It is not something that we can do as a prerequisite for salvation. If someone has a heart of stone, they plainly cannot exercise faith unless their heart has first been made into a heart of flesh. It is humbling to realize that our faith and good works are the effects of God's gracious action, not the cause. Furthermore, it is interesting to note that this promise in Ezekiel is made by Yahweh just before the prophet is taken to the valley of dry bones (Ezekiel 37), which cannot come to life except by the grace of God.

In these two passages from the prophets, we find six wonderful promises given by God to his people. First, he promises regeneration—the gift of a new nature, consisting of the law of God dwelling in the heart. Second, God promises forgiveness of sins, and third, the indwelling of the Holy Spirit. Fourth, he guarantees a universal knowledge of God among the people of Israel, implying a personal and experiential knowledge of himself (the kind of knowledge that arises out of a genuine salvation experience), not just a head knowledge of his existence. Fifth, God promises that Israel will obey him and have a right attitude towards him for ever, and finally he grants many national blessings to the people by promising that his Spirit and words will never depart from them. Israel will have a unique relationship with him as his special people.

The vision is of a nation enjoying complete security in its land, with no need to worry about threats from other nations. Abundant rainfall and food would eradicate famine and make Israel into a new garden of Eden. The cities would be rebuilt and inhabited and the nation would be completely unified. Once again, God would have his sanctuary in Israel and would dwell in the midst of his nation for ever.

For reflection

What do you need cleansing from, and for what do you need forgiveness?

Prayer

God of unconditional love,
free me from my sins and make me whole again.
Thank you that it is by the gracious working of your Spirit alone that we are saved.
May we be always mindful of this most precious gift. Amen

Prophets and prophecies

Image of the week: either The Annunciation *or*
The Nativity, *both by Arthur Hughes,*
at Birmingham City Art Gallery

God's people were the people of the law and of the
prophets. While the law provided the structure for the
customs and rules that held their society together, it is
part of the human condition that laws by themselves are
not enough to keep people on the straight and narrow
or even in the place where they long to be. And so the
voices of the prophets cut straight to the heart of the
matter: they challenged both blind obedience and wilful
disobedience as the children of Israel kept straying over
the years. The prophets were the constant reminder of
the need for mercy and justice; they were the voices of
truth that God raised up to help his people every time
they became distracted or went off on a tangent.

The message of the prophets refers constantly to
God's covenant with his people. If the prophets unani-
mously denounce Israel's infidelity towards God, it is
because of the pact of Sinai and its demands and curses,
to which the people had agreed. To keep the covenant
alive for succeeding generations, the prophets drew
out new aspects of its nature, imbuing it with fresh

emotional overtones to help explain the mutual relationship of God and his people.

The covenant made at Sinai is an encounter of love, the attentive and gratuitous love of God, calling in return for a love that will translate itself into obedience. The teaching of the book of Deuteronomy gathers the fruit of the deepening covenant experience, setting alongside the demands, the promises, and the threats of the covenant an emphasis on the love of God.

In the holy season of Advent, when we reflect on the great foretellings of the incarnation, we might sum up the message of the prophets as 'Be prepared for life-changing miracles!' Christ's birth as a baby in Bethlehem opens our eyes to the way in which God is at work in human history, shaping events for his purposes. For those with eyes to see, prophecies are being fulfilled each and every day.

Yet a tension exists between the expectation that characterizes our Advent waiting and the celebration of Christmas. While we can rejoice at the gift of the incarnation, we must still live in a state of Advent anticipation until the promise of Christ's second coming is fulfilled. Thus, to encounter the living Christ is to experience intense gratitude and joyful hope at one and the same time. To live in nothing but perpetual hope would be to deny that God has already answered our every need and given us more than we could ever have asked for; and to stop expecting Christ's coming would mean measuring God's gifts with a human yardstick.

Image of the week weblinks

http://cgfa.sunsite.dk/hughes/p-hughes13.htm
http://cgfa.sunsite.dk/hughes/p-hughes14.htm

A new shoot, a new wisdom

A shoot will spring from the stock of Jesse,
a new shoot will grow from his roots.
On him will rest the spirit of Yahweh,
the spirit of wisdom and insight,
the spirit of counsel and power,
the spirit of knowledge and fear of Yahweh:
his inspiration will lie in fearing Yahweh.
His judgment will not be by appearances,
his verdict not given on hearsay…

The wolf will live with the lamb,
the panther lie down with the kid,
calf, lion and fat-stock beast together,
with a little boy to lead them.
The cow and the bear will graze,
their young will lie down together.
The lion will eat hay like the ox.

ISAIAH 11:1–3, 6–7

The background to this famous 'lion and lamb' prophecy is God's declaration of doom on Assyria after they deported Israel. But he promises to spare Judah and Jerusalem because of the righteousness of King Hezekiah of the house of David. Our passage then sets out the promise and prophecy of the coming Messiah.

The Messiah is called different things depending on the translation but is usually a shoot, a rod or stock, and a branch. All the words signify something small and tender: a shoot is easily broken off. He emerges from the stem or stock of Jesse: when the royal family was cut down and almost levelled to the ground by its own self-destruction, it would naturally sprout again. The house of David was at an all-time low at the time of Christ's birth but, when the Messiah came, he made it clear from early on that his kingdom was not of this world and, therefore, would be more enduring.

To help in God's rescue plan for humankind, the Messiah will have the Spirit of Yahweh resting upon him. Isaiah writes that the Spirit of the Lord would 'rest' on the Messiah (v. 2); the Hebrew word here means that the Spirit would 'dwell' or 'remain' with the Messiah. We see the beginning of that process in John's Gospel when John the Baptist says of Jesus, 'I saw the Spirit come down from heaven as a dove and remain on him' (1:32, NIV). The Holy Spirit, with all God's gifts and graces, shall rest upon him, and so the Messiah will have the fullness of the Godhead dwelling in him.

We also know that we can have utter confidence in this Messiah because he will be just and righteous in all that he does. As a result, there will be great peace under his jurisdiction. Christ, the great shepherd, will take care of his flock—a theme that goes on to recur throughout the New Testament. The nature of human troubles, and even of death itself, will be utterly changed because God's people will be delivered not only from evil but also from the very fear of it.

Isaiah also sets out a vision of the future; the sublime beauty and richness of the poetry here is as dynamic as the jolting power of the images. This is a vision of paradise regained or Eden restored, but even better because it promises a person who will bring peace and salvation. Isaiah is challenging Judah: 'look how good life could be if you turn in obedience to God'. The description of strong and weak animals living together in harmony is a reminder that peace will come only when the strong look after the weak rather than dominating them. The animals could also represent the political powers at the time, with Egypt, Assyria and Babylon like the lion and the wolf, while Israel and Judah are like the vulnerable lamb or kid, at the mercy of those powers. The passage could, then, be read as promising a lasting end to hostilities between nations.

The image of the lamb, of course, has deeper significance. The spotless sacrificial lamb was offered under the Mosaic system as a way of gaining access to God and making peace with him. It recalls the Passover lamb first offered immediately before the exodus from Egypt—and, looking forward, it points to Jesus as the Lamb of God taking away the sins of the world (see John 1:29). His death on the cross provided both a sacrifice for sins and a way into God's presence.

For reflection

Is there someone with whom you need to make peace this Advent? How can you make this happen?

Prayer

God of wolves and lambs,
may I learn to live in harmony with your world.
Give me wisdom, counsel and knowledge in my daily
undertakings,
and may your Spirit rest on me in all that I do. Amen

The angel and the Spirit

In the sixth month, God sent the angel Gabriel to Nazareth, a town in Galilee, to a virgin pledged to be married to a man named Joseph, a descendant of David. The virgin's name was Mary. The angel went to her and said, 'Greetings, you who are highly favoured! The Lord is with you.' Mary was greatly troubled at his words and wondered what kind of greeting this might be. But the angel said to her, 'Do not be afraid, Mary, you have found favour with God. You will be with child and give birth to a son, and you are to give him the name Jesus. He will be great and will be called the Son of the Most High. The Lord God will give him the throne of his father David, and he will reign over the house of Jacob for ever; his kingdom will never end.'

'How will this be,' Mary asked the angel, 'since I am a virgin?' The angel answered, 'The Holy Spirit will come upon you, and the power of the Most High will over-shadow you. So the holy one to be born will be called the Son of God. Even Elizabeth your relative is going to have a child in her old age, and she who was said to be barren is in her sixth month. For nothing is impossible with God.'

'I am the Lord's servant,' Mary answered. 'May it be to me as you have said.' Then the angel left her.

LUKE 1:26–38 (NIV)

What was it that so perplexed Mary? Instead of using her name, Gabriel gave her a title, a most strange title for an ordinary peasant girl living in a town of no consequence: '*kecharitomene*'. *Kecharitomene* is sometimes translated as 'favoured' or 'full of grace' but it is more accurately translated 'You who have been and are now filled with divine favour'. No one except Mary has been greeted this way by an angel, and Gabriel uses the term only once.

The archangel Gabriel is the exalted messenger of God, whose name means both 'messenger' and 'the strength or power of God', and who in the Old Testament is recorded as helping the prophet Daniel to interpret his dream-visions. In the New Testament it is Gabriel who brings important news to Zechariah and the virgin Mary concerning the birth of their children; it is not unreasonable to suppose, along with much Christian tradition, that Gabriel also appeared to Joseph and to the shepherds, and even that it was he who 'strengthened' Jesus in the garden of Gethsemane before the crucifixion. Thus he is, throughout the biblical record, the angel of the incarnation and of consolation and, in accordance with his name, the angel of the power of God.

Next in our passage, Gabriel tells Mary that 'the Holy Spirit will come upon you, and the power of the Most High will overshadow you'. The word 'overshadow' here comes from the Greek words *epi* meaning 'over' and *skia* meaning 'a shadow'. It is similar to the word used for the bright cloud that overshadowed Christ at his transfiguration (Matthew 17:5; Mark 9:7) and also for the apostle Peter's shadow falling upon the sick in Acts 5. It resonates with the Old Testament idea of a cloud symbolizing the immediate presence and power of God, none other than the Hebrew *shekinah*.

The *shekinah* appeared to Moses on Mount Sinai (Exodus 34:5), and in the Holy of Holies, above the ark of the covenant, in the most sacred part of the Jerusalem temple (1 Kings 8:10–11). In using such a similar word for the Spirit's overshadowing of Mary, Luke is clearly drawing a parallel between God's presence in the Holy of Holies and in the very person of Mary. As we saw previously, she is the new, living tabernacle and sanctuary of God, chosen to bear the Messiah. As the conversation develops between Gabriel and Mary, she is given a number of promises and prophecies about the future role of her son.

When Gabriel said that the Holy Spirit would 'come upon' Mary, he changed her. He caused Mary to become pregnant. This was absolutely necessary in the plan of God. We know that Christ is the eternal Son of God: of course, his existence didn't begin with his birth to Mary as he was already eternal. However, Christ wanted to enter into the world as a sinless human to shed pure blood for our sins, and so he chose to be born of a woman with the help of the power of the Holy Spirit.

In this episode, Mary quite literally becomes the bearer and the beholder of our Christian salvation. She was confused as she pondered what the angel's greeting could mean, but this in itself can show us that God resides with us in silence, in stillness, in our openness and in our desire for meaning. When we are in all of these things, the Spirit can speak to us most clearly. Mary's response also reminds us that God has un-limited patience to wait for us all to say 'yes' to him, for us to agree that the events of our lives should unfold according to his word.

For reflection

Think about a time in your life when the beginning or birth of something good happened, and give thanks to God for that time.

Prayer

Creator God,
your marvels are indeed everywhere.
May we never forget that nothing is impossible with you.
Today let us hear the messengers you send us,
and respond with an eager 'Yes, Lord'. Amen

A blessing and a visit

Mary set out at that time and went as quickly as she could into the hill country to a town in Judah. She went into Zechariah's house and greeted Elizabeth. Now it happened that as soon as Elizabeth heard Mary's greeting, the child leapt in her womb and Elizabeth was filled with the Holy Spirit. She gave a loud cry and said, 'Of all women you are the most blessed, and blessed is the fruit of your womb. Why should I be honoured with a visit from the mother of my Lord? Look, the moment your greeting reached my ears, the child in my womb leapt for joy. Yes, blessed is she who believed that the promise made her by the Lord would be fulfilled.'

LUKE 1:39–45

Elizabeth would have had to reconcile herself to never having children, a great shame and sorrow in her culture, as in so many other cultures even today. To discover that she was expecting a baby in old age would have been physically shocking as well as mentally and emotionally cataclysmic, but she kept her faith in God. For her, a long, barren journey had come to an end and she had reached a new point in her life.

While Elizabeth is coming towards the end of her life, Mary is only at the beginning. While Elizabeth has wanted a baby for many long years, Mary has conceived when she least expected it. And so the two spiritual journeys of these women, although at different ends of the physical spectrum, meet in the unborn babies in their respective wombs and in the knowledge that their children are destined to change the face of human history for ever.

Mary set out into the hill country to visit Elizabeth's house. The Greek word that Luke uses to describe how Mary goes off is most evocative: *anastasa* means 'to rise'. *Anastasa* can thus recall all the moments in Israel's past when someone arose to initiate actions, particularly actions in accordance with the covenant of God, as when God commanded Abram, 'On your feet! Travel the length and the breadth of the country, for I mean to give it to you' (Genesis 13:17). The word also looks forward in anticipation toward the greatest rising up of all—the resurrection of Christ from the dead, from the shedding of blood that initiated the new and everlasting covenant that we celebrate in the eucharist.

When the angel announced to Mary that the child she was to bear would be called 'Son of the Most High', Mary gave her assent, her 'yes' to God. Then the Holy Spirit came upon her. In that moment, Mary became the first person consciously to follow Christ. With her 'yes' she participates in the very life given in Christ, and, filled with the wonder of the Spirit, she is drawn out of her home and into the hill country of Judea.

Her first act is to reach out to another person—her cousin Elizabeth—and so she rises out of her house, out of her current circumstances, to venture into a new world in which she has no map or signposts, and with only an unknown angel's assurance that she will be blessed in her surrender. Like Abraham and Sarah, she is also undertaking a colossal journey of trust.

To help her in the challenge she faces, Mary has some supportive relationships: her friendship with her cousin Elizabeth and, later, her marriage to Joseph who, reassured by the angel, offers her understanding and protection. Later still, she will find a different and more poignant friendship in John the beloved disciple, whom Jesus brings to her side just before his own death. Friendship and miracles, prophecies and simple acts of kindness are all noticeable aspects of this story. We are taught that when we, like Mary, surrender without reserve to God's will and power, then everything is possible and life will never be the same again.

For reflection

How can you be filled afresh with the Holy Spirit this Advent?

Prayer

God of life-changing visits,
let me leap with joy in anticipation of your Son's birth.
May I follow the example of Mary and Elizabeth
in yielding to the workings of your earth-shattering grace.
Amen

A rising sun

His father Zechariah was filled with the Holy Spirit and spoke this prophecy:

Blessed be the Lord, the God of Israel,
for he has visited his people, he has set them free,
and he has established for us a saving power
in the House of his servant David,
just as he proclaimed,
by the mouth of his holy prophets from ancient times,
that he would save us from our enemies
and from the hands of all those who hate us,
and show faithful love to our ancestors,
and so keep in mind his holy covenant.
This was the oath he swore
to our father Abraham,
that he would grant us, free from fear,
to be delivered from the hands of our enemies,
to serve him in holiness and uprightness
in his presence, all our days.
And you little child,
you shall be called Prophet of the Most High,
for you will go before the Lord
to prepare a way for him,
to give his people knowledge of salvation
through the forgiveness of their sins,
because of the faithful love of our God
in which the rising Sun has come from on high to visit us,

to give light to those who live
in darkness and the shadow dark as death,
and to guide our feet
into the way of peace.

LUKE 1:67–79

Zechariah was a priest and upright in the sight of God, observing all the commandments and regulations of his faith blamelessly. According to Mosaic law, priests were not required to marry a wife from the tribe of Levi (Leviticus 21:7, 13–15), but for a priest to have a wife descended from Aaron, as Elizabeth was (Luke 1:5), was considered a twofold honour. Yet Elizabeth was barren, and the honour had turned to shame. Since she was well past her childbearing years, the couple had gracefully but sorrowfully resigned themselves to the situation.

For most of the year, Zechariah and Elizabeth lived in a small village 'in the hill country of Judea', south of Jerusalem (Luke 1:39), except when Zechariah's priestly duties took him to the temple. Priests were divided into 24 groups or divisions (1 Chronicles 24: 7–18), of which Zechariah's 'division of Abijah' was eighth in the rotation. Priests and their families would live in Jerusalem or in nearby villages, but when their division was called up for duty for a week, twice each year, they would come to Jerusalem.

Each day, about 50 priests would have been on duty. One day, Zechariah was selected by lot to go and burn incense on the altar in the Holy Place, a great honour that happened to a priest only once in a lifetime. In the midst of Zechariah's prayer, an angel of God appeared and stood at one end of the altar, right in front of the priest. After 400 years of silence, with no manifestations from God, no prophetic word since Malachi, God had now sent an emissary to speak on his behalf and to promise Zechariah a son, who would bring people back to God.

Yet Zechariah did not believe it was going to happen, and so he became mute—but only until the child was born. Then his tongue was set loose and he blessed God, filled with the Holy Spirit and bursting with wondrous song. Zechariah at last comes to real faith in God's promise: his faith timetable is just a little slower than Mary's and Elizabeth's.

His song is known as the Benedictus (Latin for 'Praise be', the opening words in the Latin Vulgate translation of the Bible). It falls naturally into two parts. The first verses are a song of thanksgiving for the realization of the messianic hopes of the Jewish nation. As in former days, when there was power to defend the nation against her enemies, so now that strength would be restored to them, but in a new, spiritual sense. While the Jews had impatiently borne the yoke of Roman rule, they had continually sighed for the time when the house of David would be their deliverer. The deliverance is now at hand, and Zechariah points to this as the fulfilment of God's promise to Abraham so many centuries before; but the fulfilment is described as deliverance not for the sake of worldly power, but that we may 'serve him without fear in holiness and righteousness before him all our days' (vv. 74–75, NIV).

The second part of Zechariah's song is addressed to his own son, who is to take so important a part in the scheme of redemption; for he is to be a prophet, to preach the forgiveness of sins before the coming of the Son from on high. The prophecy that he is to 'go before the Lord to prepare a way for him' is, of course, an allusion to the well-known words of Isaiah (40:3–5), which John the Baptist himself later applied to his own mission.

So, both Zechariah and his future son John show us the way to Christ. In this time of Advent, let us follow Zechariah's prophecy with openness of heart. Let us ask God that we too may be delivered from all our fears and all that holds us down—to see that the prophet from on high is in our midst if we take time to look.

For reflection

How can you bring light to those who live in darkness this Advent?

Prayer

God of promises and prophecies,
show us your saving power in our lives today.
May we turn to your risen Son each day
and let him guide us in the way of peace. Amen

The Spirit and the fire

In due course John the Baptist appeared; he proclaimed this message in the desert of Judea, 'Repent, for the kingdom of Heaven is close at hand.' This was the man spoken of by the prophet Isaiah when he said: A voice of one that cries in the desert, 'Prepare a way for the Lord, make his paths straight!'

This man John wore a garment of camel-hair with a leather loin-cloth round his waist, and his food was locusts and wild honey. Then Jerusalem and all Judea and the whole Jordan district made their way to him, and as they were baptized by him in the river Jordan they confessed their sins. But when he saw a number of Pharisees and Sadducees coming for baptism he said to them, 'Brood of vipers, who warned you to flee from the coming retribution? Produce fruit in keeping with repentance, and do not presume to tell yourselves, "We have Abraham as our father," because, I tell you, God can raise children for Abraham from these stones. Even now the axe is being laid to the root of the trees, so that any tree failing to produce good fruit will be cut down and thrown on the fire. I baptize you in water for repentance, but the one who comes after me is more powerful than I, and I am not fit to carry his sandals; he will baptize you with the Holy Spirit and fire. His winnowing-fan is in his hand; he will clear his threshing-floor and gather his wheat into his barn; but the chaff he will burn in a fire that will never go out.'

MATTHEW 3:1–12

John's preaching is described in Luke's account as a 'baptism of repentance for the forgiveness of sins' (3:3). Previously the angel Gabriel had told Zechariah what John's ministry would be, and now here we have John declaring it for himself. The word 'repentance' has the root meaning of 'to turn': in other words, it involves a turning of the direction of our life and the affections of our heart, so that we become centred on God and love the things he loves. It is John the Baptist's task to turn as many people as he can to the Lord their God. He promises them 'forgiveness of sins' in response to their repentance, their turning to God, and he calls them to demonstrate the seriousness of their turning by accepting baptism in the Jordan river.

This was a remarkable demand for John to make. Baptism had one main significance among the Jewish people: it was the symbolic rite that proselytes had to go through to become Jewish. This made John's baptism seem very offensive. It implied that unless the Jewish people were willing to repent, they were not really Jewish and could not be guaranteed the blessings that God had promised to his chosen people. To put it another way, in calling the Jewish people to accept a baptism of repentance for the forgiveness of their sins, John was telling them that they could not rely on the practice of their Jewish faith for salvation; they had to be changed in their heart toward God.

This understanding of John's baptism could thus open the way for Gentiles to repent and be forgiven as well. If being a member of the Jewish people did not save in itself, then being a Gentile did not necessarily condemn: the issue was whether or not somebody showed repentance towards God and wanted forgiveness for their sins.

Very bluntly John tells the Pharisees and Sadducees that they are in a rotten condition: they are a 'brood of vipers' (v. 7). Interestingly, in Genesis 3 Satan is pictured as a serpent or a viper, and God says to that serpent, 'I shall put enmity between... your offspring and hers' (Genesis 3:15). To tell them that they were the offspring or the brood of a viper was the same as saying they were sons of the devil. John also warns that there is wrath on the way. God will bring judgment upon Satan and his allies. There are sons of God and sons of the viper, and the former will be gathered into the barn of heaven and the latter thrown into the fire of hell.

At Christmas, most people don't want to hear a passionate John the Baptist talking about judgment. Unquenchable fire just does not sound like good news. But John mentions that there is an escape from wrath. We can flee from it to the baptism of repentance for the forgiveness of sins. There is no more condemnation for those who repent and receive God's absolution. Repentance is turning away from any and all dependence on what I am by birth (such as Jewish or Gentile) or what I have done by my own efforts, towards the absolutely free mercy of God for the hope of salvation, open to us all if we are ready to accept it.

Lastly, it is significant that John is identified as a 'voice of one that cries in the desert' (v. 3). We may often feel as if we are wandering in the desert, abandoned or neglected by those we love and even by God. There is another way to think about such 'wilderness experience'. In order to develop a closer relationship with God, we sometimes actually need to be in the desert—to be free from daily distractions so that we can focus on him, away from our usual lives so that we can be silent and listen. Only then will we be able to hear God's voice calling us.

For reflection

What do you most need to repent of this Advent?

Prayer

God of spirit and fire,
cleanse me from my sins and purify my heart.
Help me to produce good and lasting fruit
and kindle your unquenchable fire of love within me. Amen

The Lord is here

Image of the week: The Light of the World *by Holman Hunt, in St Paul's Cathedral and Keble College, Oxford*

When the early Christians called Jesus 'Lord', it wasn't only a religious statement but also a political one, because they were challenging the Roman emperor's claims to divine authority on earth. It is important to remember that the political structures in Hebrew and Roman times were just as confusing, corrupt and exploitative as they can be in the world today. And just as it is easy to think only in terms of our own country's politics and overlook the bigger picture, so it was in Israel and in Rome for those struggling to find their political place in society. Yet we see that the prophets intervened constantly in the political affairs of their kings to remind them of their duty to the people. We can see Jesus as a very political leader who challenged the authorities constantly but retained a balanced view in the management of church and state; he knew what belonged to Caesar and what belonged to God (Matthew 22:20–21).

We tend to think that life today, in our fast-paced and globally-minded world, is more dangerous and fragile than in past times. We are bombarded with issues—terrorism, the AIDS pandemic, global poverty and environmental damage—and we can sometimes end up numbed to the reality behind the words. We can forget the devastating impacts that they have on the lives of ordinary people and on the planet itself, and, if we dwell on them too much, we can end up despairing at the scale of the problems facing us all.

It would be wrong, though, to imagine that biblical times were any less precarious. Like so many today, people in the Old and New Testaments had to contend with the threat of conflict, whether locally or between nations. There were slavery, poverty, appalling health problems (no NHS or emergency medical supplies) with high infant and maternal mortality rates; they endured flood, plague, famine, exile.

Christians in any age must be conscious of their calling to act in society too, whether working in the religious or political sphere. And one further question that never goes away, and with which people have always wrestled, is how, in practice, authority can be reconciled with freedom, and personal initiative with the needs of the whole social framework. While both religious groups and political parties can work to support whatever in their opinion is conducive to building a better society, the temptation remains to put their own interests before the common good.

All citizens must play their part in religious and political affairs. They must combat injustice and oppression, random domination and intolerance by individuals or groups, and they must do so with integrity and wisdom.

This is what the Old and New Testaments teach us time and time again. And we have the example of Jesus to follow: one led by service to others, not as a doormat but as a leader who had each person's interests at heart.

Image of the week weblinks

www.explore-stpauls.net/oct03/textMM/LightWorldN.htm

www.keble.ox.ac.uk/about/chapel/chapel-history-and-treasures

Holy is his name

And Mary said:

My soul proclaims the greatness of the Lord
and my spirit rejoices in God my Saviour;
because he has looked upon
the humiliation of his servant.
Yes, from now onwards
all generations will call me blessed,
for the Almighty has done great things for me.
Holy is his name,
and his faithful love extends age after age
to those who fear him.
He has used the power of his arm,
he has routed the arrogant of heart.
He has pulled down princes from their thrones
and raised high the lowly.
He has filled the starving with good things,
sent the rich away empty.
He has come to the help of Israel his servant,
mindful of his faithful love
—according to the promise he made to our ancestors—
of his mercy to Abraham
and to his descendants for ever.

Mary stayed with [Elizabeth] some three months and then
went home.

LUKE 1:46–56

This song or canticle is Mary's response to the mystery of the annunciation: the angel had invited her to rejoice and Mary now expresses the exultation of her spirit in God her Saviour. Her joy flows from the personal experience of God's looking with kindness upon her, a person with no historical influence. The word *Magnificat*, the Latin version of a Greek word with the same meaning, celebrates the greatness of God, who reveals his omnipotence through the angel's message, surpassing the expectations and hopes of the people of the covenant, and even the highest aspirations of the human soul.

In the presence of the powerful and merciful God, Mary expresses her own sense of lowliness and humility (v. 48). The Greek word used recalls the 'humiliation' and 'misery' of a barren woman (see 1 Samuel 1:11) who confides her pain to the Lord. With a similar expression, Mary makes known her situation of poverty and her awareness of being little before God, who by a free decision looked upon her, a humble girl from Nazareth, and called her to become the mother of the Messiah.

The words describing how all generations will call Mary blessed follow on from Elizabeth's proclamation that her cousin was 'blessed'. Not without daring, the song predicts that this same proclamation will be extended and spread abroad with ever-increasing momentum, At the same time, it testifies to the special veneration for the mother of Jesus that has been present in the Christian community from the very first century.

'For the Mighty One has done great things for me—holy is his name. His mercy extends to those who fear him, from generation to generation' (v. 49, NIV). What are the 'great things' that the Almighty accomplished in Mary? The expression appears in the Old Testament to indicate the deliverance of the people of Israel from Egypt, Assyria and Babylon. In the Magnificat, it refers to the mysterious event of Jesus' virginal conception, which occurred in Nazareth after the angel Gabriel's announcement.

The Magnificat reveals that not only is God the Almighty to whom nothing is impossible, as Gabriel had declared, but he is also most merciful, capable of tenderness and faithfulness towards every human being. Overturning the judgments of the world, he comes to the aid of the poor and lowly, to the detriment of the rich and powerful, and in a surprising way he fills with good things the humble who entrust their lives to him. The song furthermore exalts the generous fulfilment of God's promises to his chosen covenant people.

Inspired by the Old Testament, the Magnificat surpasses the prophetic texts on which it is based, revealing in her who is 'highly favoured' the beginning of a divine intervention that far exceeds Israel's messianic hopes: the holy mystery of the incarnation of the Word. The words of this song help us to understand that it is especially humility of heart that attracts God's kindness. It is a song of promises and prophecies whose fulfilment we celebrate this and every Christmas.

We are told that Mary stayed with Elizabeth for three months before she came home again. Could it be that

Mary helped at the birth of the forerunner of her own child, the one who had come to prepare the way for the Saviour?

For reflection

Where in your church and community do you most need to work to bring about justice?

Prayer

God of justice and love,
may we stop our endless talk about justice
and start living it day by day.
From this moment on,
help us to take action and not just work with words. Amen

The Word became flesh

The Word was the real light
that gives light to everyone;
he was coming into the world.
He was in the world
that had come into being through him,
and the world did not recognize him.
He came to his own
and his own people did not accept him.
But to those who did accept him
he gave power to become children of God,
to those who believed in his name
who were born not from human stock
or human desire
or human will
but from God himself.
The Word became flesh,
he lived among us,
and we saw his glory,
the glory that he has from the Father
as only Son of the Father,
full of grace and truth.

JOHN 1:9–14

To a much greater extent than in the other three
Gospels, the whole of John's Gospel centres around
the person of Jesus, the redeemer. From his opening

sentences, John turns his gaze to the innermost recesses of eternity, to the divine Word of the Father. He continually focuses on the dignity and glory of the Christ who promised to live among us, so that, while receiving this extraordinary revelation, we might also participate in the fullness of his grace and truth.

As evidence of the Saviour's credentials, John charts some of the great wonders by which Christ revealed his glory, yet he is far keener to lead us to a deeper understanding of Jesus' divinity and majesty by a reflection on his words and teaching, and to impress upon our minds the glorious marvels of his unconditional love.

These verses introduce the themes and recurring ideas found elsewhere in John. God is the Word to us: he is divine and eternal; he created all things, and is the source of our being and of life itself. John then makes a shocking statement that the world failed to recognize him (v. 10). The light who came to bring life was unrecognized, even by his own people. The world rejected its Creator, ruler and sustainer.

This rejection recalls the way the Israelites rejected God throughout their history, but it also relates to us, when we turn away from God or do not believe in him. Those who do believe and receive the Word are given the immediate and absolute right to belong to God. This isn't something that happens naturally—we can't understand the light—but it comes about through the action of God's grace. Amazingly, God has made it possible for us to be part of his family. Then comes another bombshell. The Word is God in human flesh and has made God known. This 'making God known' is the fulfilment of all that the Old Testament pointed towards. The phrase 'he lived among us' (v. 14)—literally, 'pitched his tent among us'—goes right back to the book of Exodus, when God dwelt among his people in a tent in the wilderness (Exodus 29:45–46).

John says that the Word's revelation was like this: God lived among us—but as a human being. His use of the word 'glory' (v. 14) reminds us of Moses' request to see God's glory. Moses could not see God and live, but God passed in front of him, proclaiming his compassion and grace, justice and righteousness (Exodus 33:18; 34:4–7). In claiming to have seen his glory, 'the glory of the One and Only… full of grace and truth' (1:14, NIV), John is claiming to have seen even more than Moses did. He has seen the compassion and justice of God in human flesh.

The phrase 'grace and truth' actually comes from the Old Testament and is translated in the Greek Old Testament as 'mercy and truth'. It describes the covenant mercy of God, his gracious constancy, his dependable kindness toward his people. Jesus, the incarnate Word, radiates this kindness, this grace. In past times, the people of Israel knew something of God's loving kindness, particularly in the law, but his enduring grace in Christ transcends all that has been before.

There is something wondrous about God's grace. Jesus reveals the grace of God, and in that revelation we witness the glory of God, we confront the divine. On recognizing the truth, we receive it, and it changes us. Grace and truth might seem miles away from today's politics but, as they were part of the Christmas mystery

2000 years ago, they continue to challenge us even more today.

For reflection

Why didn't the world recognize Jesus, and how will you recognize him this Advent?

Prayer

God of grace and truth,
you came to us in glory
and we failed to see you.
When you come again and all creation sees your glory,
may we be ready to welcome you
and let your glory live among us. Amen

Christ is born

Now it happened that at this time Caesar Augustus issued a decree that a census should be made of the whole inhabited world. This census—the first—took place while Quirinius was governor of Syria, and everyone went to be registered, each to his own town. So Joseph set out from the town of Nazareth in Galilee for Judea, to David's town called Bethlehem, since he was of David's House and line, in order to be registered together with Mary, his betrothed, who was with child. Now it happened that, while they were there, the time came for her to have her child, and she gave birth to a son, her first-born. She wrapped him in swaddling clothes and laid him in a manger because there was no room for them in the living-space.

LUKE 2:1–7

Joseph is one of scripture's unsung heroes, always in the background and allowing others to take the limelight. Yet without him, what would have become of Jesus and his mother? In what we read of Joseph, we can find a powerful model for fathering and step-fathering for today's world.

Joseph plays only a small part in the New Testament, appearing only in the Gospels of Matthew and Luke, and mentioned as Jesus' father in John. He protects the infant Jesus through Mary's pregnancy and, following the birth, protects the baby from Herod by the dramatic action of smuggling the family out of the country. Later he is revealed as provider, bringing them back into Israel, yet continuing to be alert in his role as protector by settling not in Judea, but further north, in Nazareth. In order to fulfil these roles of protector and provider, Joseph needed to know when he was being prompted by God; in the opening chapters of Matthew, he recognizes God speaking to him in four different dreams.

As the one whose task it was to parent Jesus, Joseph had an awesome task! Yet it is clear that he fulfilled the role of an earthly father, committing himself completely to the upbringing of the child for whom God had given him responsibility. Joseph the carpenter was fundamental to God's plan for his Son's birth but would never be a prominent or acclaimed figure.

In the midst of Joseph's faith journey was the political reality into which the Christ-child would be born: the earthly government exercised its seemingly limitless power through a decree that the whole world must be counted and registered by name. But counting and naming are the prerogatives of God alone: 'He determines the number of the stars and calls them each by name' (Psalm 147:4). Who was the Emperor Augustus to set himself up as a god? He was so unimportant in relation to the child who was to be born, and yet at this moment in history he appeared to be the one pulling the strings. There is a strange irony at work here. And yet God used this occasion to fulfil the words of his prophets. For now, Joseph was obliged to travel with his wife to Bethlehem, where Micah prophesied that the one who was to rule in Israel would be born (Micah 5:2).

In that town, Mary gave birth to Jesus, of whom the prophet Isaiah had written, 'dominion has been laid on his shoulders' (9:5). Only God has the power to control our destiny, and what is amazing is that he doesn't exercise that power. Out of love God invites us, calls each of us by name. He will never force his faithful ones to do anything.

Two very different events coincide during the month of December. There is a secular holiday called 'Christmas' that has almost nothing to do with the birth of Jesus in Bethlehem. This holiday involves buying gifts, preparing special foods, decorating and putting up an evergreen tree. The whole month of December is given over to this winter festival. Meanwhile, there is the real Christmas—quieter, hidden behind the winking lights and torn wrapping paper.

The commercial Christmas itself hungers for more than can be supplied by warmth and cheer alone. It hops from party to party, exhausting itself in excess until it collapses on New Year's Day with a false promise to do better, go on a detox diet and stop shopping until the next salary cheque appears. But for us the child has only just been born. We await his first steps, his first words, his flowering into adulthood. In Christ, even now, we are always beginning anew. We make no resolutions. We merely remain with our hands open, contemplating the gift that grows in wonder, through no effort of our own.

For reflection

Where is God's power at work in your life?

Prayer

God our Saviour,
we thank you for the birth of your only Son.
We marvel at your most precious gift to us,
and cherish this new present in humble adoration.
Today you have turned all our sunsets into dawns. Amen

Just as they had been told

In the countryside close by there were shepherds out in the fields keeping guard over their sheep during the watches of the night. An angel of the Lord stood over them and the glory of the Lord shone round them. They were terrified, but the angel said, 'Do not be afraid. Look, I bring you news of great joy, a joy to be shared by the whole people. Today in the town of David a Saviour has been born to you; he is Christ the Lord. And here is a sign for you: you will find a baby wrapped in swaddling clothes and lying in a manger.' And all at once with the angel there was a great throng of the hosts of heaven, praising God with the words: Glory to God in the highest heaven, and on earth peace to those he favours.

Now it happened that when the angels had gone from them into heaven, the shepherds said to one another, 'Let us go to Bethlehem and see this event which the Lord has made known to us.' So they hurried away and found Mary and Joseph, and the baby lying in the manger. When they saw the child they repeated what they had been told about him, and everyone who heard it was astonished at what the shepherds said to them. As for Mary, she treasured all these things and pondered them in her heart. And the shepherds went back glorifying and praising God for all they had heard and seen, just as they had been told.

LUKE 2:8–20

There are so many things we don't know about Mary and Joseph. How long was their journey from Nazareth to Bethlehem? What did they speak about along the way? We don't even know if Mary was able to ride a donkey, as artists through the centuries have assumed, or whether she had to walk the entire way to the city of David.

We wish to know these lost details because we love Mary, Joseph and Jesus. We long to accompany them on every step of their journey. If only we could see through their eyes, hear what their ears heard! Love makes us desire this knowledge, but there is another sort of love, a love that averts its gaze and blushes in the presence of the beloved.

In fact, the most beautiful and meaningful experiences are always hidden. Much as we love them, Mary and Joseph are not our property. In the face of their human dignity, we take a step back and acknowledge that our own greatest, highest moments of existence don't and can't take place on a stage.

Luke never records the moment when Jesus was conceived or the particular details of his human birth, and his passage from death to the risen life is 'buried' for ever behind a large stone. These are mysterious and holy events upon which we cannot and must not trespass. And yet, in this life we experience our own personal conceptions, our own private births, our own mysterious conversions, when the truth of the resurrection of Christ takes hold of us and transforms us. Most particularly in the eucharist, we live the whole history of salvation and enter into the deepest mysteries of Christ's life. In this way, God allows us to draw near to the secrets that lie veiled at the heart of the gospel.

The Lord God himself is a shepherd who feeds and waters his own sheep, dresses their wounds, names them, knows them and searches for them when they wander. When human shepherds undertake these same responsibilities, they can't help but participate in God's nature. Even if the shepherds in Bethlehem did not appreciate the sacred dimension of their work, their everyday duties would have slowly conformed them even a little to the image of God.

Christ's coming is for all peoples in every nation and from every class. The story of the shepherds illustrates this, as they were a despised and powerless group and yet were the first to visit Christ. The Christ-child is also powerless but, through his powerlessness, ultimately overcomes all the great powers of evil. Jesus began his life with the despised and the lowly; he ended his life on the cross with the despised and lowly thieves. So the Christ-child is made manifest not through his own power initially but through the witness of his people. The shepherds' faithful witness as the first who are poor in spirit provides us with a wonderful context in which to share Christ today.

Here we have a lesson in God's attitude to the marginalized, to those outside traditional hierarchies, whose social status is of little account. Just as he values them enough to make them the first to hear the good news, so we must value those who are smaller, weaker or poorer than we are. When we do that, we stand on holy ground.

For reflection

What can the shepherds teach you about how you see God?

Prayer

God of shepherds and sheep,
thank you for tending us
especially when we stray.
May we learn to see all people with your loving eyes
and may we be your loving arms as we care for them. Amen

Touched with our own hands

Something which has existed since the beginning,
which we have heard,
which we have seen with our own eyes,
which we have watched
and touched with our own hands,
the Word of life—
this is our theme.
That life was made visible;
we saw it and are giving our testimony,
declaring to you the eternal life,
which was present to the Father
and has been revealed to us.
We are declaring to you
what we have seen and heard,
so that you too may share our life.
Our life is shared with the Father
and with his Son Jesus Christ.
We are writing this to you
so that our joy may be complete.

1 JOHN 1:1–4

By the time John wrote his first epistle, many errors regarding what it meant to be a Christian were threatening the expanding Church. So, with a pastoral heart, John writes to encourage his readers that they can have assurance of their salvation. This assurance, he believes, is based upon understanding three things: obeying God, believing the truth about who Jesus is, and loving and living with others faithfully.

The prologue to 1 John introduces us to a number of themes, particularly the importance of eyewitness testimony about Jesus, his earthly ministry as a part of God's revelation of himself, and the eternal life available to all believers in Jesus. By the time John's epistle was written, a heresy called gnosticism had begun to emerge. This taught that the physical, material world was evil and only the immaterial, intangible world was divine. The divine could never become human—and the divine Son of God certainly could not have been fully human. John wanted his readers to know that this teaching was false and that his own physical witness to the 'Word of life' was conclusive proof that the Son of God was both material and divine reality.

John also assures his readers, including us, that the truth about salvation is grounded in the personal and historical, the perceiver and the perceived, the experience and the experienced. In case we forget that experiencing and proclaiming Christ are merely a means to an end, though, John reminds us that God is bringing about his objective in our salvation.

John states two purposes for proclaiming the Word of life: fellowship and joy (vv. 3–4, NIV). 'Fellowship', or sharing in a close union with others, depends entirely upon a relationship with God through Christ. It is impossible to have genuine biblical fellowship with other believers and not have fellowship with God through his Son Jesus (and vice versa). Christians are related to one another as a branch is related to a vine. We are all part of a spiritual family.

Biblical 'joy' is a quiet, inner confidence that our salvation is secure. It is not surprising that our greatest joy is often in the giving of ourself to other people. It is in and through encounters with others that we are most enriched; this is why John emphasizes the sharing of testimony about the new relationship available to everyone in Christ. It is not a private enterprise, a private joy, just for the select few, but something in which we can all participate. To share in this testimony is to share in God's love, to experience a bonding in faith with each other and with Christ, and this is something that will bring us complete joy.

In the West, we take more or less for granted the fact that we can share the truth, enjoying free speech and freedom to witness to our faith unharmed and without ridicule. In many parts of the world, people are killed for their beliefs and for daring to speak out their ideas. How can they share the testimony and the Word of life when their own life is in danger? How on earth can their joy be complete under such persecution? This Christmas, we would do well to ponder with thanks on how our faith can be lived out freely and to think about how we can help other Christians to do the same. Mary, Joseph and the magi had to be very careful at the time of Jesus' birth, because Herod was trying to stop them (Matthew 2:13): we still have Herods today, persecuting Christians for the same faith, but we can make a difference—if we are prepared to do so.

For reflection

Is there someone with whom you can share your faith in Jesus Christ this Christmas?

Prayer

God of all our senses,
show us how to hear, see, touch and taste
your mighty Word of life.
And when we do, help us to share it happily,
so that our joy may be complete in you. Amen

A new life in Christ

Image of the week: The Adoration of the Magi,
attributed to Zanobi Strozzi,
National Gallery, London

Jesus Christ is not confined to the New Testament. His coming was anticipated by men and women who lived before the New Testament books were written: 'A feeling of expectancy had grown among the people, who were beginning to wonder whether John [the Baptist] might be the Christ' (Luke 3:15). Running through the Old Testament, a divine 'watermark' predicts and reveals the nature of Israel's coming Messiah. This first part of the Bible isn't just God's message to the Jewish people or an account of their history. For Jesus himself, these scriptures explained his birth, the work he was to accomplish, and the glory awaiting him and all those who come to God through him. Our understanding of Christ is diminished if we do not discover him in the Old Testament scriptures as well as the Gospels and letters of the New Testament.

The Old Testament foretold that the Messiah would be Jewish, born in Bethlehem in the royal line of David the king, of the tribe of Judah. These are clear and detailed prophecies. Solomon was the immediate successor of David, but he was not born in Bethlehem. He certainly built a temple for God, but his throne was not established for ever. Micah's prophecy, about the Messiah being born in Bethlehem (5:2), was written at least 200 years after the death of David. About 700 years later, Jesus was born in Bethlehem, a few miles from Jerusalem in the land of Judah.

The wonderful message of Jesus Christ gave comfort and healing to ordinary men, women and children, and they were astonished at his teachings. All kinds of people, high and low, rich and poor, sick and healthy, came to him and were cradled in his words of care and salvation. This was exactly what the Old Testament prophets had foretold of him: 'The spirit of Lord Yahweh is on me for Yahweh has anointed me. He has sent me to bring the news to the afflicted, to soothe the broken-hearted, to proclaim liberty to captives, release to those in prison, to proclaim a year of favour from Yahweh' (Isaiah 61:1–2).

Jesus' miracles were not simply the extension of his teachings; they were living evidence that he was Son of God, bringing to men, women and children a foretaste of the kingdom of heaven. The climax of Jesus' life was his crucifixion, foretold a thousand years before he was even born. His resurrection, the final miracle that crowned everything that had gone before, came to his followers as a joyful surprise, even though it too was foretold.

Jesus used the Old Testament prophecies as powerful evidence when he spoke to the apostles after his resurrection: '"Everything written about me in the Law of Moses, in the Prophets and in the Psalms, was destined to be fulfilled." He then opened their minds to understand the scriptures' (Luke 24:44–45). These are significant words. Jesus took his followers back to the three main parts of the Old Testament—the books of Moses, the Prophets and the Psalms. He showed how in those scriptures there were truths that were fulfilled in his own life-story.

After his resurrection, Jesus also commanded the apostles to go out as his witnesses to preach the gospel throughout the world. As part of their preaching, they used those same messianic prophecies: the history of Jesus written before it happened. Jesus Christ is the bridge between Eden and the promised glorious end. He is the means by which God fulfils his mission of mercy and salvation. Those Old Testament prophecies are part of the story of God's great plan of redemption. The covenant, which dominated all human history, finds its culmination in Christ.

In his birth Jesus was wrapped in swaddling clothes but in his second coming he will be wrapped with a robe of light. His life on earth culminated in his sufferings on the cross and his death; one day he will return in glory with his angels. The Jesus who ascended to heaven is the Christ who is coming again to reign on earth as King of kings and Lord of lords. He who wore the crown of thorns will wear the crown of glory. Those promises will be fulfilled as surely as the prophecies about his first coming were fulfilled on that first Christmas.

Image of the week weblink

www.nationalgallery.org.uk (and search "Adoration of the magi")

A great light and a great gift

The people that walked in darkness
have seen a great light…
For a son has been born for us,
a son has been given to us,
and dominion has been laid on his shoulders;
and this is the name he has been given,
'Wonder-Counsellor, Mighty-God,
Eternal-Father, Prince-of-Peace.'

ISAIAH 9:1a, 5

This passage seems contradictory, as it comes between two stern warnings of judgment. It is an oracle of hope and deliverance, which looks to the future when there will be no oppression and when peace will reign. The oppression that the people of Judah and Jerusalem suffered was both physical and spiritual—physical in that the Assyrians dominated and subjugated them and spiritual in that they also feared death and the darkness of doubt. Despite the many attempts by Yahweh and his prophets to show them how they must live and the kind of faith they should have, the Israelites couldn't quite trust in the God who had already saved them countless times. Thus here Isaiah is describing the coming of the Christ-child who will lead them to freedom, who will be their real king, their everlasting light.

This passage must have been enormously significant

in raising morale and confidence in a nation that was torn and fragmented. It is an amazing prophecy because it speaks about the birth of a child who will come to help the Israelites in their time of greatest need and in their greatest weakness, thereby demonstrating God's power and authority. It seems strange that a child would be wise, a counsellor, almighty, but all would be made clear in the coming of the Saviour-King, 700 years later.

God takes the initiative, giving us his Son, his very self, freely. God is for us, given to us, and he is Emmanuel, too—God with us. When we begin to sense the truth about God's astonishing generosity, it deepens our longing to remain in his presence and serve him. And it is only through him, with him and in him that we can offer him the one thing he desires: our entire selves, our lives.

Nestled in the manger we see the shepherd king, son of David and Son of God, who offers himself as a gift. Completely vulnerable and helpless before his chosen flock, he is very much as he will be at the moment when he gives himself up to be nailed to the cross. Even at the moment of his birth, the rough wood of the manger foreshadows the rough wood of the cross, and the bands of cloth in which Mary so carefully wraps her child foretell the linen bands used to wrap his body for burial. His birth at Bethlehem contains the seed of his glorious rebirth in the resurrection.

God's generosity comes with no strings attached, no bargains, no commercial transactions. With divine patience, he waits for a response from us. May we receive the grace to see his goodness, and may we, full of adoration and praise, let go of our human wishes enough to love him with our whole hearts.

There are other gifts that God gives to us to help us in our walk of faith: people whom he sends us, to be unwrapped and treated as precious. Some of these gifts are not enveloped in beautiful paper with exciting ribbons; some are so badly wrapped that if we only considered the outside we would miss the richness inside. Some are packaged so tightly, others too loosely, while others arrive quite damaged and broken. What we are called to do is look with God's eyes, to see the true worth and ponder what response such a gift requires.

For reflection

Can you think of someone whom God may have sent into your life as a gift, to show you something of himself?

Prayer

God of light and gifts,
thank you for giving me your Son.
In times of light and darkness
may I remember this most precious gift,
and cherish Christ with all my heart. Amen

Love is strong

Flowers are appearing on the earth.
The season of glad songs has come,
the cooing of the turtledoves is heard in our land…

Set me like a seal on your heart,
like a seal on your arm.
For love is strong as Death,
passion as relentless as Sheol.
The flash of it is a flash of fire,
a flame of Yahweh himself.
Love no flood can quench,
no torrents drown.
Were a man to offer all his family wealth
to buy love,
contempt is all that he would gain.

SONG OF SONGS 2:12; 8:6–7

The Song of Solomon, also known as Song of Songs and Canticles, is a sequence of lyric poems celebrating human love. The poetry is graceful, sensuous and replete with erotic imagery and allusions. It features the voices of two lovers, one male and one female, and their professions of love for one another. At times the two voices join in dialogue but at others they speak separately. Christian tradition also developed a symbolic or allegorical interpretation, reading the Song as an account of Christ's love for the Church and later as an expression of the soul's spiritual union with God.

The seal mentioned here could be worn bound to the arm, suspended round the neck or as a ring (see Jeremiah 22.24). It was used for identification and signatures, and, since it was unique to its owner, the use of it as an image in the poem is a request to belong to the beloved alone. Alternatively, it could refer to an imprint made by rolling a cylinder on wet clay, speaking of the desire to leave a permanent impression on the heart. Either way, the verses describe enduring love, the reality of jealousy and the fact that love cannot be bought.

Love, which is as certain of its victory as are death and Sheol (a term used for the underworld, the realm of the dead), matches its strength against the natural enemies of life: waters cannot extinguish it or floods carry it away. It is more priceless than all riches. Nothing can compare in power with a love that transcends death.

Human love should not be seen as separate from divine love. The rich imagery evokes many different facets of love between humans—and love between God and his creation. The image of the seal can indeed remind us of God's covenant with us, as well as our covenant with those we love. The love of Jesus, made incarnate at Christmas, is the highest love of all. Whether between a man and a woman or between God and us, love is about listening, watching and longing. It is about seeing potential in the most unlikely of situations and knowing that we can rejoice and sing even in the midst of suffering and death.

The Song allows the beloved to be mysterious and,

at the same time, someone with whom we may be intimately involved. Our Lord is veiled in infinite mystery but, at the same time, we may move eternally into an ever-deeper relationship with him. The infinite identity of God, like that of the beloved in the Song, is found only in the most intimate involvement with him, and the signs of this involvement are exultation and rejoicing, a mutual outpouring of joy and delight.

The Song of Songs tells in vivid poetry how a bridegroom and bride rejoice over and delight in each other. Christ's love is far stronger than any human emotion. His love is eternal and transcends suffering, poverty, even death itself. On the day of our salvation, our Lord and Saviour will rejoice and delight over us and we in him.

For reflection

What or whom do you love most in life, and why?

Prayer

God of love,
you who are stronger than death,
who have conquered Sheol,
may your love seal our hearts
and quench all our sorrows. Amen

An unknown day and hour

'As it was in Noah's day, so will it be when the Son of man comes. For in those days before the Flood people were eating, drinking, taking wives, taking husbands, right up to the day Noah went into the ark, and they suspected nothing till the Flood came and swept them all away. This is what it will be like when the Son of man comes. Then of two men in the fields, one is taken, one left; of two women grinding at the mill, one is taken, one left.

'So stay awake, because you do not know the day when your master is coming. You may be quite sure of this, that if the householder had known at what time of the night the burglar would come, he would have stayed awake and would not have allowed anyone to break through the wall of his house. Therefore, you too must stand ready because the Son of man is coming at an hour you do not expect.'

MATTHEW 24:37–44

We are warned here that no one except God knows exactly when the parousia, the second coming of Christ, will arrive. In Greek, *parousia* meant 'appearance and subsequent presence with' and in the ancient world it referred to official visits by royalty. It was then appropriated by Christians as a unique term for Jesus' glorious return at the end of history.

The passage reminds us of Noah, who believed in Yahweh and built the ark in faith, but even when the flood came many people were surprised, as they had not prepared themselves or centred their hearts on God. Watchfulness for the will of God is crucial, and we should not get so caught up in our daily lives that we fail to see and understand God's signs for his world.

Advent is a time of preparation for Christ's coming, and every year many of us will come to Christmas feeling that we haven't spent enough time just being with God. If we are too busy to pray, then we are too busy. And we must make sure we are ready for the day when the Son of man will come again.

Every time we pray the Lord's Prayer, we pray that God's kingdom may come, and that God's will may be done. Through repeating these familiar words, we can become immune to the power of what we are praying. Yet this longing for the coming of the Lord is an important aspect of Advent. Yes, we celebrate his birth at Christmas with our carols and nativity scenes, but we still await the second coming of Jesus our Saviour. He has promised to return.

The Bible passage calls us to be watchful and alert to the will of God, nurturing our relationship with God, prepared for his coming. While Matthew is asking us to think about the 'end time', we also need to be watchful for God's action in our everyday lives. Just as in Noah's day, we can ignore warning signs and get on with our lives. We may feel self-sufficient and see no place for God in our lives: we're just too busy! But if we are alert to God, then we never need feel truly despairing, even if our world seems to be collapsing around us.

Someone once said, 'Remember yesterday, plan for tomorrow, but live for today.' If we thought that today was our last day on earth, we would live differently. We would manage our relationships carefully and we would put God at the centre of all that we do. We can 'stay awake' by reflecting on how we live our lives and asking ourselves whether we live as Jesus would want us to do. As God loves us so completely, it is only a matter of stopping in our busyness and taking a breath to know that God is there with us and longs for us to respond to him.

For reflection

How can you be more watchful in your faith during the year to come?

Prayer

God of Noah and of me,
help me not to grow weary of watching and waiting.
Give me hope and courage
to stand ready for your return,
no matter how long I have to wait in your love. Amen

A frightened king

After Jesus had been born at Bethlehem in Judea during the reign of King Herod, suddenly some wise men came to Jerusalem from the east asking, 'Where is the infant king of the Jews? We saw his star as it rose and have come to do him homage.' When King Herod heard this he was perturbed, and so was the whole of Jerusalem. He called together all the chief priests and the scribes of the people, and enquired of them where the Christ was to be born. They told him, 'At Bethlehem in Judea, for this is what the prophet wrote:

> And you, Bethlehem,
> in the land of Judah,
> you are by no means the least
> among the leaders of Judah,
> for from you will come a leader
> who will shepherd my people Israel.'

Then Herod summoned the wise men to see him privately. He asked them the exact date on which the star had appeared and sent them on to Bethlehem with the words, 'Go and find out all about the child, and when you have found him, let me know, so that I too may go and do him homage.' Having listened to what the king had to say, they set out.

MATTHEW 2:1–9a

Herod had a kind of faith: he believed that a 'king' would come and rule Israel, but his faith was very different from that of the magi. His faith made him fear this king and want to kill him, not worship him. There are enormous struggles between power and fear in these Christmas scriptures—warnings not just of Jesus' precarious position but of the powers that will battle over his ministry later in life, that will lead to his death.

Herod embodies the prophecy that people will not believe in Jesus, that they will be afraid of his power and, in their weakness and fear, will send him to his death (Isaiah 53). Herod is afraid of the truth of the incarnation. He is terrified as he sees his own identity eclipsed by the coming of a greater person with a radically different kingship. He does not want a Saviour who will change the world. He does not want a Saviour to forgive his sins. He wants things just as they are, with him in control. An old, tyrannical and paranoid king, fearing that this newborn baby will threaten the power he wants to hand down to his sons, becomes the catalyst for the massacre of the innocent children of Bethlehem. King Herod sought to kill Jesus while the magi came to worship, bearing expensive gifts.

The magi went first to the king's palace when they arrived after their long journey. What splendour they must have seen! This was surely where they would find the new king. Yet, in the end, the star led them to the place where Jesus was to be found and there they found no crown, no riches or splendour. Indeed, there was no evidence of royalty at all, other than the witness of the star.

So what was it that the magi believed? They believed that the 'king of the Jews' was born. He was to be worshipped because he was divine and they had no problem believing in his miraculous birth. They rejoiced greatly and worshipped the child Jesus as soon as they saw him, giving him the gifts that they had brought as suitable for a king (2:11).

The prophet Micah, whose words are quoted in our passage, lived towards the end of the eighth century BC, one of the most traumatic periods of Old Testament history. The Assyrian empire was on the rise, forcing the frightened states of Syria, Israel and Judah to take drastic defensive action. By the end of the century, Israel would have fallen to Assyria and Judah would be all but overrun. The overriding issue that dominated every-body's lives was that of security in a world of insecurity, especially for the people of God. It was difficult to know whom they should trust, and even their earthly leaders were less than trustworthy. It was at this point that Micah received his prophecy of a Messiah who would bring peace.

It was not just Herod, however, who had no idea that the Saviour of the world had been born. Jesus' birth would have passed almost unnoticed. Few grasped the meaning of this cataclysmic event and others were troubled by it. But there were some, like Mary and Joseph, the shepherds and the magi, who saw with the eyes of faith. They looked beyond appearances and saw the reality. They understood the event in terms of the Old Testament scriptures and in the light of the revelations given at the time of the birth. They believed the truth and believed in him, kneeling before a baby in worship. We too can do the same, this year and every year.

For reflection

What do you think your response would have been to the birth of Jesus—fear or worship?

Prayer

God of majesty and humility,
may our faith in you be bold;
may our fears be small,
and our delight shine like the magi's star.
From east to west and north to south,
you are our Saviour,
now and for eternity. Amen

The star of delight

I see him—but not in the present.
I perceive him—but not close at hand:
a star is emerging from Jacob,
a sceptre is rising from Israel,
to strike the brow of Moab,
the skulls of all the children of Seth.

NUMBERS 24:17

And suddenly the star they had seen rising went forward and halted over the place where the child was. The sight of the star filled them with delight, and going into the house they saw the child with his mother Mary, and falling to their knees they did him homage. Then, opening their treasures, they offered him gifts of gold and frankincense and myrrh. But they were given a warning in a dream not to go back to Herod, and returned to their own country by a different way.

MATTHEW 2:9b–12

At the time of Moses, the wicked king Balak summoned a man named Balaam from the east, requiring that he place a curse on the Israelites. Instead, Balaam blessed them and prophesied that a star would rise out of Jacob. And now, in Jerusalem, magi come from the east with news of a star. Another wicked king plots to destroy the hope of Israel. If, instead of asking where the Messiah was to be born, Herod has asked his advisers to explain the meaning of this new star, he might have heard the prophecy of Balaam and understood himself as in the role of Balak. And what might have happened then?

Biblical history doesn't repeat itself; rather, certain moments of heightened intensity point ahead to moments of even greater glory. Each time a theme resurfaces in salvation history, God reveals more details of his cosmic plan and the total picture comes into better focus. The evil that exists in the world does not change. Each time it expresses itself in history, it is the same darkness, but light gathers luminosity and shines more brightly in each succeeding generation. If you compare Balaam's star to the star of the magi, the first star is a promise, while the second is an indication of fulfilment. Balaam's star symbolized victory for the Israelites' army, but the star of the magi pointed to the victory by Christ in conquering sin and death.

The angels and the star each announce the incarnation. Through the Gospels, both celestial messengers proclaim the good news of great joy to us now, where we are, today. Yet, for us, there is more. We ourselves can experience the living Christ in light, touch and see him in water and oil, and taste him in bread and wine. Through these sacramental gifts, he transforms us, along with our brothers and sisters, so that we encounter him in one another as well.

The magi had come a long way, and now what stood before them? An ordinary door to an ordinary house situated in an ordinary town. Yet now they knew that their exhausting journey was over. With unshakeable conviction, they understood that their heart's desire was within reach, that every promise would be kept and every prayer answered. In a flash, one fact had communicated all these things and more: they saw that the star had stopped.

The magi gazed in deep wonder at what they found: heaven on earth, earth in heaven, humanity in God, God in humanity, one whom the whole universe could not contain now enclosed in a little body. As they looked, they believed and did not question, as their symbolic gifts bear witness: incense for God, gold for a king, myrrh for one who is to die.

Like them, we stand at the threshold, and we know very well what waits for us behind the door. We glimpse a reality that is endless, a mystery with no final definition, no limit—and quite spontaneously we know that the only appropriate response is to offer ourselves. This knowledge comes to us through God's grace and inspiration and not through any intellectual processes. Yet, upon reflection, our hearts confirm that when we offer ourselves, we participate in God's essential nature.

The good shepherd gives the sheep all they need, even to the point of laying down his own life. In fact, without his prior gift, we would be incapable of giving anything. But through him, with him and in him, we do give ourselves, along with all the gifts he has ever given to us, and in this way we prolong our joy and enter more profoundly into relationship with the author of all joy.

For reflection

Imagine that you are following a star in search of Jesus. Where do you think it would lead you?

Prayer

God of Advent, Christmas and Epiphany,
you have given us many promises and prophecies
about your Son Jesus Christ's birth,
and they have been fulfilled.
May we see from the past to the present,
the present to the future,
and know that your loving hand guides all things. Amen

Journey to Jerusalem

Bible readings from Ash Wednesday to Easter Sunday

David Winter

'Twelve young men were walking with their leader along a road about 30 miles north of Galilee, in a hilly area where the river Jordan had its source. As they walked, their leader put two questions to them, and the answer to the second one would have profound consequences not just for them but eventually for the whole world. The leader was Jesus. The twelve young men (and they were young, most of them barely in their 20s) were his disciples.'

This book follows the journey of Jesus and his followers to Jerusalem—the story of the culmination of his ministry in the events of Good Friday and Easter, the story of the 'good news of God' for the whole world. As we reflect on these events, like the disciples we can experience the awakening of faith in Jesus and hear the challenge to follow him, wherever he leads.

ISBN 978 1 84101 485 2   £7.99
Available from your local Christian bookshop or, in case of difficulty, direct from BRF using the order form on page 127.

Beginnings and Endings
[and what happens in between]

Daily Bible readings for Advent and Christmas

Maggi Dawn

Advent is all about beginnings. It's the beginning of the Church year, and its themes include the beginning of creation, the beginning of Christianity, and the beginning of the new heavens and the new earth. Most of these beginnings are born out of the ending of something else—an old era giving way to a new one.

Our everyday lives are full of small-scale beginnings and endings—births, deaths, marriages, careers, house moves and so on. This book reflects on the stories of six groups of people and individual characters from the Bible; each provides a focus in some way for the idea of beginnings and endings, and each gives us a glimpse into—and draws ancient wisdom from—the human experience that happened in between.

ISBN 978 1 84101 566 8   £7.99
Available from your local Christian bookshop or, in case of difficulty, direct from BR using the order form on page 127.

ORDER FORM

REF	TITLE	PRICE	QTY	TOTAL
458 2	Journey to Jerusalem	£7.99		
566 8	Beginnings and Endings	£7.99		

POSTAGE AND PACKING CHARGES					Postage/packing:	
order value	UK	Europe	Surface	Air Mail	Donation:	
£7.00 & under	£1.25	£3.00	£3.50	£5.50	**Total enclosed:**	
£7.01–£30.00	£2.25	£5.50	£6.50	£10.00		
Over £30.00	free	prices on request				

Name _____ Account no _____

Address _____

_____ Postcode _____

Tel. _____ Email _____

Total enclosed £ _____(cheques made payable to 'BRF')

Payment by: cheque ❑ postal order ❑ Visa ❑

Mastercard ❑ Switch ❑

Card no: ☐☐☐☐☐☐☐☐☐☐☐☐☐☐☐☐☐☐☐☐

Expires ☐☐☐☐ Security code ☐☐☐ Issue no ☐☐☐

Signature (essential if paying by credit/Switch card) _____

All orders must be accompanied by the appropriate payment.

Please send your completed order form to:
BRF, First Floor, Elsfield Hall, 15–17 Elsfield Way, Oxford OX2 8FG
Tel 01865 319700 / Fax 01865 319701
Email: enquiries@brf.org.uk

❑ Please send me further information about BRF publications.

Available from your local Christian bookshop.   BRF is a Registered Charity

brf

Resourcing your spiritual journey

through...

- Bible reading notes
- Books for Advent & Lent
- Books for Bible study and prayer
- Books to resource those working with under 11s in school, church and at home

- Quiet days and retreats
- Training for primary teachers and children's leaders
- Godly Play
- Barnabas

For more information,
visit the **brf** website at **www.brf.org.uk**